Franciscan Virtues through the Year

52 STEPS TO CONVERSION FROM SAINT FRANCIS OF ASSISI

Confraternity of Penitents

ISBN: 1530146976
ISBN 13: 9781530146970

Prayer of Saint Francis before the Crucifix of San Damiano

Most High, glorious God,
enlighten the darkness of my heart
and give me true faith,
certain hope and perfect charity,
sense and knowledge, Lord,
that I may carry out
Your holy and true command.

Franciscan Virtues through the Year: 52 Steps to Conversion from Saint Francis of Assisi is published by the Confraternity of Penitents, copyright 2016.

Members of the Confraternity of Penitents live, in their own homes as married and single laity, a modern adaptation of the original Rule, which Saint Francis of Assisi gave to the penitent lay people in the year 1221. The Confraternity invites the reader to visit the Confraternity website at www.penitents.org for more information.

ORDER INFORMATION

Franciscan Virtues through the Year is sold through the Confraternity of Penitents Holy Angels Gift Shop, an on line Catholic book and gift shop at www.cfpholyangels.com

Mail order from the Confraternity of Penitents Holy Angels Gift Shop, 1702 Lumbard Street, Fort Wayne IN USA 46803, 260/739-6882

$10.95 plus shipping and handling

Table of Contents

Introduction

How can we have Franciscan virtues? Aren't all virtues virtuous? How could some virtues be Franciscan and others not be?

Truly all virtues are Franciscan virtues. St. Francis intended to follow Jesus, and Jesus taught us to follow Him by practicing the virtues. The Franciscan virtues are those virtues which St. Francis of Assisi specifically embraced in his life.

This study is intended to take you through the year by studying one virtue per week. If you are a member of a Franciscan Order, your Order may wish to use these virtues as part of your formation process. They may have another time frame for studying the virtues. Each virtue contains specific suggestions for you to follow so that you can understand how the virtue is implemented in your Order's Rule and Constitutions.

You will notice how brief the reflections are. This is because the Holy Spirit must be your primary instructor as you study and practice the virtues. Each reflection contains quiet meditative time on the virtue and a series of questions to prompt your dialog with the Holy Spirt. May you be a receptive student!

In order to complete this study, you will need a Bible, particularly the New Testament. You will also need a journal which can be a simple notebook, preferably with lined paper. If you are a member of a Religious Order, you will also need a copy of your Rule of Life and Constitutions.

Acknowledgements

Franciscan Virtues through the Year was written by several members of the Confraternity of Penitents. These include Joel Whitaker, Lucy Fernandez, Rhea Schoettner, Ann Fennessey, and Madeline Pecora Nugent. In addition to these writers, other members proofread parts of the manuscript. These include Eric Kumalec, Gretchen Everin, Michael Megery, Reji Kurian, Ben Douglass, Maria Deliz, Tammy Ringhand, Dianne Joslyn, Colleen Nazareth, Karen Bianco, and Kimberly Lohman. CFP member Jennifer Vetter edited the final manuscript. Thanks to each of these members for their contributions, work, and prayers.

We thank New City Press for their permission to quote Francis' writings and incidents from their Early Document series (Francis of Assisi: Early Documents, Volumes 1, 2, 3, published by New City Press, copyright 1999). Quotes not from New City Press are from Fr. Pascal Robinson's translation of the lives and writings of Saint Francis. These are readily available on the internet.

We thank artist Tim Luncsford for designing the cover of this book.

Franciscan Virtues through the Year

52 STEPS TO CONVERSION FROM SAINT FRANCIS OF ASSISI

CHAPTER 1

Attentiveness

Scripture
"Keep awake, therefore, for you know neither the day nor the hour." (Matthew 25:13)

Writings of Saint Francis
"Reflect and see that the day of death is approaching. With all possible respect, therefore, I beg you not to forget the Lord because of this world's cares and preoccupations and not to turn away from His commandments, for all those who leave Him in oblivion and turn away from His commandments are cursed and will be left in oblivion by Him." (Saint Francis of Assisi, A Letter to the Rulers of the Peoples, 1220)

Incident from the Life of Saint Francis
One time when blessed Francis was at that same place, a certain brother, a spiritual man, an elder in religion, was staying there. He was very sick and weak. Considering him, blessed Francis was moved to piety towards him. The brothers back then, sick and healthy, with cheerfulness and patience took poverty for abundance. They did not take medicines in their illnesses, but more willingly did what was contrary to the body. Blessed Francis said to himself: "If that brother would eat some ripe grapes early in the morning, I believe it would help him."

One day, therefore, he secretly got up early in the morning, and called that brother and took him into the vineyard which is near that same church. He chose a vine that had grapes that were good and ready for eating. Sitting down with that brother next to the vine, he began to eat some grapes so that the brother would not be ashamed to eat alone, and while they were eating them, that brother praised the Lord God.

As long as he lived, he always recalled among the brothers, with great devotion and flowing tears, the mercy the holy father had done to him. (The Assisi Compilation, Section 53)

HAVE YOU EVER typed a response to someone in an email while chatting on your phone to someone else?

St. Francis never had this temptation, but this is a good example of someone lacking the virtue of attentiveness. Attentiveness is a broad virtue. It means not only paying attention to the person to whom we are speaking, but also paying attention to whatever task we are doing or whatever ministry God has given us to perform. Attentiveness means attention to God in prayer, without letting our minds be distracted about other things. It means focusing on God and seeing all things in relation to Him. This is the message that Francis was trying to get across to all the governing authorities of his day. He was telling them not to be so caught up in the things of this world that they seldom if ever paid attention to spiritual matters and their final demise. It was just as easy in Francis's day as it is today to get caught up in matters of the world and to forget about God, or to put Him aside until we have "more time."

Spend a minimum of five minutes meditating on the Virtue of Attentiveness. Do not write anything during this time. Merely begin your time by praying, "Lord, help me to understand the Virtue of Attentiveness and where I need it in my life."

At the end of your meditation time, ask yourself:

Who or what needs my attention? Am I attentive to that person and that situation? If so, how am I attentive? If not, how can I become more attentive?

Am I attentive to how God is moving in my life? If so, how am I attentive to this? If not, how can I do better?

Find another section in Scripture which illustrates the Virtue of Attentiveness. Find a statement of Jesus or an incident in His life that deals with the Virtue of Attentiveness. Write these into your journal.

If you are a member of a Religious Order, find one place in your Rule or Constitutions which calls for the Virtue of Attentiveness. Explain why you chose this section.

Practice the Virtue of Attentiveness this week. Record in your journal any memorable insights or happenings.

Each evening, examine your day for the times when you were attentive and for the times when you lacked attentiveness. Pray each night, "Lord, make me attentive to Your Presence and Your actions in my life, in the lives of others, and in the world around me. Amen."

At the end of the week, record in your journal what you have learned from this exercise.

Chapter 2

Confession

Scripture

If we confess our sins, he is faithful and just and will forgive us our sins and purify us from all unrighteousness. (1 John 1:9)

Writings of Saint Francis

Let all my blessed brothers, both clerics and lay, confess their sins to priests of our religion. If they cannot, let them confess to other discerning and Catholic priests, knowing with certainty that, when they have received penance and absolution from any Catholic priest, they are without doubt absolved from their sins, provided they have humbly and faithfully fulfilled the penance imposed on them. (The Earlier Rule, Chapter XX)

Incident from the Life of Saint Francis

One day, although still sick from a quartan fever, he had the people of Assisi called to the piazza for a sermon. When he had finished preaching, he requested that no one leave until he returned. . . . Taking off his tunic, blessed Francis ordered Brother Peter to lead him naked with a rope tied around his neck in front of the people. He ordered another brother to take a bowl full of ashes and, mounting the place from where he had preached, to throw them and sprinkle them on his head. . . . In this way he came back in front of the people naked, to the place where he had preached, and said: "You believe me to be a holy man, as do others who, following my example, leave the world and enter the religion and life of the brothers. But I confess to God and to you that during my illness I ate meat and broth flavored with meat." Almost all the people began to weep out of piety and compassion for him, especially since it was wintertime and was very cold and he had not yet recovered from the quartan fever. They struck their breasts, accusing themselves. "This holy man," they said, "whose life we know, accuses himself with such shame over a just and manifest necessity. Yet because of excessive abstinence and the severity with which he treats his body from the moment of his conversion to Christ, we see him living in flesh that is almost dead. What shall we do, wretches that we are, we who all our life have lived, and wish to live, according to the will and desires of the flesh?" (The Assisi Compilation, Section 80)

CONFESSION IS A sacrament as well as a virtue. In this reflection, we are discussing confession as a virtue rather than a Sacrament. Sacramental confession is made to a priest who gives absolution for sins and assigns a penance for them. The virtue of confession urges us to confess to others, possibly often.

Do you remember your first confession? It may not have been in church in the confessional. You may have had to confess to stealing a cookie or breaking a toy when you were just a youngster. Confession is often a humiliating experience. We have to admit to someone else that we did something wrong, when more than anything we want to believe that we are perfect, and we want bring others to that same belief. Confession is a great way to acknowledge that we are far from perfect.

The toddler who steals cookies or breaks a toy has been caught in the act of doing something wrong, but many times we can do wrong secretly. When we sin in secret, no one knows but God. Most often we confess these things to the priest in the privacy of the confessional. Yet notice how St. Francis confessed to the general public what he considered to be secret sins, even though the food he ate was necessary for his health.

We often refrain from confessing to others because we still think like the toddler--we want to be perfect, and we want others to think that we are perfect, even though we know we are not. What are you hiding from others that should be confessed to them? Is it difficult to say, "I made a mistake on that; I forgot that; I have been ignoring you; I am too self-centered?"

Spend a minimum of five minutes meditating on the Virtue of Confession. Do not write anything during this time. Merely begin your time by praying, "Lord, help me to understand the Virtue of Confession and where I need it in my life."

At the end of your meditation time, ask yourself:

What do I need to confess? Who do I need to confess to? Should I confess to them? When can I do this? Why am I afraid to confess to someone? What can I do about my fears?

Find another section in Scripture which illustrates the Virtue of Confession. Find a statement of Jesus or an incident in His life that deals with the Virtue of Confession. Write these into your journal.

If you are a member of a Religious Order, find one place in your Rule or Constitutions which calls for the Virtue of Confession. Explain why you chose this section.

Practice the Virtue of Confession this week. Record in your journal any memorable insights or happenings.

Each evening, examine your day for the times when you confessed or should have confessed to another. Evaluate why you did or did not confess and how you felt. Pray each night, "Lord, help me to acknowledge my weaknesses to myself and to others and to know that You, and probably others, will forgive me. Please help me to forgive myself. Amen."

At the end of the week, record in your journal what you have learned from this exercise.

CHAPTER 3

Courage

Scripture
Wait for the LORD, take courage; be stouthearted, wait for the LORD! (Psalm 27:14)

Writings of Saint Francis
[T]he Lord says: "Behold I am sending you like sheep in the midst of wolves. Therefore, be prudent as serpents and simple as doves." That any brother, then, who desires by divine inspiration to go among the Saracens and other nonbelievers, go with the permission of his minister and servant. If he sees they are fit to be sent, the minister may give them permission and not oppose them, for he will be bound to render an accounting to the Lord if he has proceeded without discernment in this and other matters. (The Earlier Rule, Chapter XVI)

Incident from the Life of Saint Francis
Although at the time battles were being fought between the Christians and the unbelievers every day, trusting in the Lord he was not afraid to approach the Sultan even at clear peril to his life. After being afflicted with numerous heavy blows and insults, he finally gained a personal audience with the Sultan. (The life of St. Francis by Julian of Speyer, Chapter VII)

COURAGE IS NOT foolhardiness. Courage is the ability to do something that frightens one, and to react with strength in the face of pain or grief. Courage makes difficult things bearable. With courage, we can find a certain joy in the midst of suffering or fear when we acknowledge that God is with us. St. Francis recognized that his Friars would have to have this sort of courage if they were going to go into dangerous situations. Sometimes, we find ourselves in dangerous or trying situations which come upon us without our consent. In these times, our courage comes from waiting for God's grace and trusting in His mercy.

Spend a minimum of five minutes meditating on the Virtue of Courage. Do not write anything during this time. Merely begin your time by praying, "Lord, help me to understand the Virtue of Courage and where I need it in my life."

At the end of your meditation time, ask yourself:

Do I consider myself a courageous person? Why or why not? Do other people consider me to be courageous? Why or why not? Who do I see as courageous? Why would I call that person courageous? How can I imitate their virtues? Do I want to imitate them? Do I want to be courageous? If not, why not?

Find another section in Scripture which illustrates the Virtue of Courage. Find a statement of Jesus or an incident in His life that deals with the Virtue of Courage. Write these into your journal.

If you are a member of a Religious Order, find one place in your Rule or Constitutions which calls for the Virtue of Courage. Explain why you chose this section.

Practice the Virtue of Courage this week. Record in your journal any memorable insights or happenings.

Each evening, examine the day for the opportunities you had to show courage. If you cannot remember any opportunities, ask God to show you. Pray, "Lord, I am not as courageous as I would like. Please develop the virtue of courage in me. Please help me to keep my eye on You, and not on myself. Help me to know that You walk with me and that You are holding me up through my day. Let me lean on Your strength and take courage from that. Amen."

At the end of the week, record in your journal what you have learned from this exercise.

Chapter 4

Courtesy

Scripture

They are not to insult anyone or be argumentative. Instead, they are to be gentle and perfectly courteous to everyone. (Titus 3:2)

Writings of Saint Francis

Blessed is the servant who, after being reprimanded, agrees courteously, submits respectfully, admits humbly, and makes amends willingly. (Admonitions, XXIII)

Incident from the Life of Saint Francis

From these stepping stones of natural strengths, he was brought to that grace that prompted him to look within himself: "You are generous and courteous to those from whom you receive nothing except passing and worthless approval. Is it not right that, on account of God who repays most generously, you should be courteous and generous to the poor?" From that day he looked on poor people generously and provided them affluently with alms. Although a merchant, he was a very flamboyant squander of wealth. One day when he was in the shop where he was selling cloth, totally absorbed in business of this sort, a poor man came in, begging alms for the love of God. Preoccupied with thoughts of wealth and the care of business, he did not give him alms. Touched by divine grace, he accused himself of great rudeness, saying: "If that poor man had asked something from you for a great count or barren, you would certainly have granted him his request. How much more should you have done this for the King of Kings and the Lord of all!" Because of this incident, he resolved in his heart, from then on, not to deny a request to anyone asking in the name of so great a Lord. (The Legend of the Three Companions, Chapter 1)

ANOTHER NAME FOR courtesy is politeness. This seems like a virtue often infrequently practiced today. We tend to notice the times when people were discourteous rather than courteous. Why is this? Is our focus on the rudeness we were shown any indication that we ourselves are not courteous? Perhaps we avoid our own conscience by seeking to focus on the faults of others. Courtesy goes beyond holding the door open for an elderly person or a woman. Courtesy involves patience with people who annoy us, take up our time, or ask what seem to be foolish questions. St. Francis realized that he was not being courteous when he refused alms to a poor man when he would have given them to someone of a higher social class. Do we treat everyone the way we would treat our boss? What does that tell us about courtesy?

Spend a minimum of five minutes meditating on the Virtue of Courtesy. Do not write anything during this time. Merely begin your time by praying, "Lord, help me to understand the Virtue of Courtesy and where I need it in my life."

At the end of your meditation time, ask yourself:

Am I a courteous person? What makes me think this? What areas of my life need more courtesy? How do I treat discourteous people? How do I react in the face of rudeness? What makes me discourteous? What can I do to change how I respond?

Find another section in Scripture which illustrates the Virtue of Courtesy. Find a statement of Jesus or an incident in His life that deals with the Virtue of Courtesy. Write these into your journal.

If you are a member of a Religious Order, find one place in your Rule or Constitutions which calls for the Virtue of Courtesy. Explain why you chose this section.

Practice the Virtue of Courtesy this week. Record in your journal any memorable insights or happenings.

Each evening, examine the day for the opportunities you had to show courtesy. Pray, "Lord, I am not always courteous. Help me to realize that my lack of courtesy comes from my abundance of pride and self-centeredness. Help me to desire this virtue of courtesy, Lord. Help me to pattern myself after our Blessed Mother, who was courteous to all. Amen."

At the end of the week, record in your journal what you have learned from this exercise.

CHAPTER 5

Detachment

Scripture

'Therefore I tell you, do not worry about your life, what you will eat or what you will drink, or about your body, what you will wear. Is not life more than food, and the body more than clothing?' (Matthew 6:25)

Writings of Saint Francis

I did "not come to be ministered unto, but to minister," says the Lord. 4 Let those who are set above others glory in this superiority only as much as if they had been deputed to wash the feet of the brothers; and if they are more perturbed by the loss of their superiorship than they would be by losing the office of washing feet, so much the more do they lay up treasures to the peril of their own soul. (Admonition 4)

Incident from the Life of Saint Francis

One of the brothers, a spiritual man, to whom blessed Francis was very close, was staying in a hermitage. Considering that if blessed Francis came there at some time he would not have a suitable place to stay, he had a little cell built in a remote place near the place of the brothers, where blessed Francis could pray when he came. After a few days, it happened that blessed Francis came. When the brother led him to see it, blessed Francis said to him: "This little cell seems too beautiful to me. But if you want me to stay in it for a few days, have it covered inside and out with ferns and tree branches."

That little cell was not made of stonework but of wood, but because the wood was planed, made with hatchet and ax, it seemed too beautiful to blessed Francis. The brother immediately had it changed as blessed Francis had requested.

For the more the houses and cells of the brothers were poor and religious, the more willingly he would see them and sometimes be received as a guest there. As he stayed and prayed in it for a few days, one day, outside the little cell near the place of the brothers, a brother who was at that place came to where blessed Francis was staying. Blessed Francis said to him: "Where are you coming from, brother?" He told him: "I am coming from your little cell." "Because you said it is mine," blessed Francis said, "someone else will stay in it from now on: I will not." (The Assisi Compilation, Section 57)

DETACHMENT IS A virtue which allows us to enjoy the good things of life without being upset if we lose them. We might call detachment the "virtue of the open hand." We need to hold everything loosely so that, should we lose something or someone, we are willing to let it go. Detachment goes beyond getting upset when someone breaks our favorite vase. People who possess the virtue of detachment can love other people dearly. They pray for them intensely. The hurts of others become their own pain, because of their compassion. The joys of others exhilarate them with happiness. Detachment does not mean caring less about others. It means caring about them in view of God's eternal plan for their lives.

People who approach life with detachment may deeply appreciate the possessions, abilities, and resources which they have. They enjoy life and live it to the full. However, they additionally possess a peace that permits them to endure loss or damage to anything or anyone without losing faith in God or losing hope in the future. God asks that we be attached to only God Himself. He is the unchanging eternal Love.

Spend a minimum of five minutes meditating on the Virtue of Detachment. Do not write anything during this time. Merely begin your time by praying, "Lord, help me to understand the Virtue of Detachment and where I need it in my life."

At the end of your meditation time, ask yourself:

What am I attached to in my life? What would devastate me if it were lost or damaged? How do I feel about the significant people in my life? How does detachment fit in with love? Do I feel that detachment is important? What is frightening about detachment? What can I do to foster detachment in myself? Should I do this?

Find another section in Scripture which illustrates the Virtue of Detachment. Find a statement of Jesus or an incident in His life that deals with the Virtue of Detachment. Write these into your journal.

If you are a member of a Religious Order, find one place in your Rule or Constitutions which calls for the Virtue of Detachment. Explain why you chose this section.

Practice the Virtue of Detachment this week. You might select one thing or way of doing things that you are attached to and work on being more detached from it. Record in your journal any memorable insights or happenings.

Each evening, examine the day for the opportunities you had to show detachment. Pray, "Lord, I am too attached to _____ (name what you are attached to). I need to be more detached from this. Please help me to hold this with a light touch and to realize that my life will not crumble if this is damaged or removed. Help me to understand that I should be only attached to You, Lord, and that You have power over everything in my life. Help me to give my life and all that I have to You. Amen."

At the end of the week, record in your journal what you have learned from this exercise.

Discernment

Scripture

Give your servant therefore an understanding mind to govern your people, able to discern between good and evil; for who can govern this your great people? (1 Kings 3:9)

Writings of Saint Francis

And when God gave me brothers, no one showed me what I should do, but the Most High revealed to me that I should live according to the form of the holy gospel. (Testament)

Incident from the Life of Saint Francis

The saint [Francis] told him [Bernard]: "We will go to the church early in the morning and, through the book of the Gospels, we will learn how the Lord instructed his disciples."

Rising at daybreak, then, together with another man named Peter, who also wanted to become a brother, they went to the church of San Nicolo next to the piazza of the city of Assisi. They entered for prayer, but, because they were simple, they did not know how to find the passage in the gospel about renunciation. They prayed devoutly that the Lord would show them his will on opening the book the first time.

Once they had finished prayer, blessed Francis took the closed book and, kneeling before the altar, opened it. At its first opening, the Lord's counsel confronted them: If you wish to be perfect, go, sell everything you possess and give to the poor, and you will have a treasure in heaven.

Blessed Francis was overjoyed when he read this passage and thanked God. But since he was a true worshiper of the Trinity, he desired it to be confirmed by a threefold affirmation. He opened the book a second and a third time. When he opened it up the second time he saw: Take nothing for your journey, etc., and at the third opening: If any man wishes to come after me, he must deny himself, etc.

Each time he opened the book, blessed Francis thanked God for confirming his plan and the desire he had conceived earlier. After the third divine confirmation was pointed out and explained, he said to those men, Bernard and Peter: "Brothers, this is our life and rule and that of all who will want to join our company. Go, therefore, and fulfill what you have heard." (The Legend of the Three Companions, Section VIII)

DISCERNMENT IS THE virtue that helps us to know the best course of action and to understand the truth and falsity in a situation. St. Francis used one method of discernment as he was determining how to live a life of penance and conversion. Note that his discernment involved both his own desires and God's will, which Francis discerned through prayer and through Scripture.

When discerning anything, the best place to begin is with prayer. Ask God to show you the right way, the right decision, the perfect action, the truth of the situation. Consulting Scripture may help you make a decision and can give insight. Speaking to others who would have the knowledge and insight to advise you is an important part of discernment. Writing down the pros and cons of each alternative can help you visually determine what might be the best course of action. Writing can also help you determine where the truth lies in a certain situation. In moral and theological situations, consulting the teachings of the Church will help you to know which decisions and courses of action are morally and theologically correct. After doing these things, you must make a decision and take action as the men did who first followed Francis. Discernment without action is useless.

Can we ever be positive that we have discerned accurately? Sometimes we cannot be certain. However, if we have asked God for His direction and have tried to prudently follow where He is leading, then we need to trust our decision.

In time we may have to discern again, but life in this world is one of continual discernment and refinement of action until we enter into eternity with God.

Spend a minimum of five minutes meditating on the Virtue of Discernment. Do not write anything during this time. Merely begin your time by praying, "Lord, help me to understand the Virtue of Discernment and where I need it in my life."

At the end of your meditation time, ask yourself:

Do I have a discerning nature? How do I discern? Am I impulsive? If so, how can I control my impulsiveness? How does discernment fit into the spiritual life? What can I do to foster better discernment? What do I need to discern at this time? What techniques can I use in my discernment?

Find another section in Scripture which illustrates the Virtue of Discernment. Find a statement of Jesus or an incident in His life that deals with the Virtue of Discernment. Write these into your journal.

If you are a member of a Religious Order, find one place in your Rule or Constitutions which calls for the Virtue of Discernment. Explain why you chose this section.

Practice the Virtue of Discernment this week. If you are not discerning any major decisions or actions, then select smaller decisions to discern such as what to eat, what to wear, or what to do for recreation. Have you ever discerned these before or did you simply act impulsively? Pay attention to any changes in your attitude or response to these decisions as you take time to discern. Record in your journal any memorable insights or happenings.

Each evening, examine the day for the opportunities you had to practice discernment. Pray, "Lord, help me to recognize the opportunities for discernment in my life. Grant me the grace to slow down and to evaluate and pray before acting or deciding. Guide me to people who can help me discern. Help me always to seek Your guidance as I discern, because I want to follow Your Will, not my own. Amen."

At the end of the week, record in your journal what you have learned from this exercise.

Chapter 7

Eagerness

Scripture

That very night the believers sent Paul and Silas off to Beroea; and when they arrived, they went to the Jewish synagogue. These Jews were more receptive than those in Thessalonica, for they welcomed the message very eagerly and examined the scriptures every day to see whether these things were so. (Acts 17:10-11)

Writings of Saint Francis

Make many copies of the other letter I am sending you, in which it is written that the praises of God be proclaimed among the peoples and in the piazzas, to give to mayors, consuls and rulers, and distribute them with great zeal to those to whom they should be given. (The Second Letter to the Custodians)

Incident from the Life of Saint Francis

A little later, hurrying to Morocco to preach the faith of Christ to Miramamolin and his court, several times he rushed on so impetuously that, intoxicated by the Spirit, he left his traveling companion behind, racing ahead all by himself. He reached Spain in a fever of eagerness, but because the Lord, who for the sake of the salvation of many others ordained otherwise, afflicted him with serious ailments so that he returned to Italy. (The Life of Saint Francis by Julian of Speyer, Chapter VII)

MOST PEOPLE WOULD not think of eagerness and virtue in relationship to each other, but eagerness truly is a virtue. Think of asking your children to perform a task. If they eagerly go about it, doesn't that delight you? When you have something to do, or somewhere to go, or someone to meet, your attitude is critical. If you are eager to do, or to go, or to meet, that eagerness and excitement will influence the people around you and make them also eager and excited. Eagerness makes difficult things easy and brings joy to those experiencing eagerness through the eager person.

People who are eager want to do something very badly. They are highly interested and have a keen expectancy regarding the task at hand. Eagerness makes everything easier to handle and to do. Only a despondent person would not want to be around an eager person. People who are eager bring out the best in us because we are drawn along by their enthusiasm. Oh, that all Christians might be eager to spread the faith!

St. Francis was extremely eager to follow Christ and to help others to do the same. Did you know that we do not have any recorded sermons of St. Francis? We only have a few letters that he wrote, his Rule and Testament, and some prayers and Canticles. Even though we do not know what he actually said, we do know that he captivated audiences and sparked conversion in many people who heard him speak. It may be that his manner of speaking and exhorting the people was so zealous and eager that people remembered his tone and emotions rather than his actual words. Perhaps his eagerness is spawned conversion in those who heard him. If this poor little man was so enthusiastic upon following Jesus in total poverty and simplicity, would not I, who have more things and less humility, not want to do the same?

Spend a minimum of five minutes meditating on the Virtue of Eagerness. Do not write anything during this time. Merely begin your time by praying, "Lord, help me to understand the Virtue of Eagerness and where I need it in my life."

At the end of your meditation time, ask yourself:

Would people call me eager to follow Jesus and to do His will? Am I eager about anything? If so, what is it? If I do not see myself as an eager person, what adjective would describe me and my attitude? Do I consider this to be a positive adjective or not? What do I need to be more eager about? How can I foster eagerness in this area? Do I think that praying for an eager attitude will benefit me? Why or why not?

Find another section in Scripture which illustrates the Virtue of Eagerness. Find a statement of Jesus or an incident in His life that deals with the Virtue of Eagerness. Write these into your journal.

If you are a member of a Religious Order, find one place in your Rule or Constitutions which calls for the Virtue of Eagerness. Explain why you chose this section.

Practice the Virtue of Eagerness this week. Pick one thing, person, or duty that you are not particularly eager about. Take some time reflecting on how you can become more eager. If you are not really eager, practice doing what you would do if you were actually eager. See how your attitude is affected by an actual or pretended eagerness. How are those around you affected? Did your attitude actually become more eager after a week of this exercise? Record in your journal any memorable insights or happenings.

Each evening, examine the day for the opportunities you had to practice eagerness. Pray, "Lord, I could use more eagerness in my life in many areas. Increase my enthusiasm for doing things Your way, for doing things that need to be done, for meeting people who do not particularly excite me. Lord, help me to see my life through Your eyes, for You have eagerly made me and You eagerly call me to holiness. Help me to be eager for You. Amen."

At the end of the week, record in your journal what you have learned from this exercise.

CHAPTER 8

Empathy

Scripture

For though I am free with respect to all, I have made myself a slave to all, so that I might win more of them. To the Jews I became as a Jew, in order to win Jews. To those under the law I became as one under the law (though I myself am not under the law) so that I might win those under the law. To those outside the law I became as one outside the law (though I am not free from God's law but am under Christ's law) so that I might win those outside the law. To the weak I became weak, so that I might win the weak. I have become all things to all people, so that I might by any means save some. I do it all for the sake of the gospel, so that I may share in its blessings. (1 Corinthians 9:19-23)

Writings of Saint Francis

Blessed is the man who bears with his neighbor according to the frailty of his nature as much as he would wish to be borne with by him if he should be in a like case. (Admonitions 18)

Incident from the Life of Saint Francis

One time in the very beginning, that is, at the time when blessed Francis began to have brothers, he was staying with them at Rivo Torto. One night, around midnight, when they were all asleep in their beds, one of the brothers cried out, saying: "I'm dying! I'm dying!" Startled and frightened all the brothers woke up.

Getting up, blessed Francis said: "Brothers, get up and light a lamp." After the lamp was lit, blessed Francis said: "Who was it who said, 'I'm dying.'"

"I'm the one," the brother answered.

"What's the matter, brother?" blessed Francis said to him. "Why are you dying?"

"I'm dying of hunger," he answered.

So that that brother would not be ashamed to eat alone, blessed Francis, a man of great charity and discernment, immediately had the table set and they all ate together with him. This brother, as well as the others, were newly converted to the Lord and afflicted their bodies excessively.

After the meal, blessed Francis said to the other brothers: "My brothers, I say that each of you must consider his own constitution, because, although one of you may be sustained with less food than another, I still do not want one who needs more food to try imitating him in this. Rather, considering his constitution, he should provide his body with what it needs. Just as we must beware of overindulgence in eating, which harms body and soul, so we must beware of excessive abstinence even more, because the Lord desires mercy and not sacrifice."

And he said: "Dearest brothers, great necessity and charity compelled me to do what I did, namely, that out of love for our brother we ate together with him, so that he wouldn't be embarrassed to eat alone. But I tell you, in the future I do not wish to act this way because it wouldn't be religious or decent. Let each one provide his body with what it needs as our poverty will allow. This is what I wish and command you." (The Assisi Compilation, 50)

EMPATHY, THE ABILITY to understand and feel the emotions of the other person, is a tremendous virtue to possess. The Native American proverb, "Never criticize a man until you have walked a mile in his moccasins," puts into concrete terms the virtue of empathy. Think about this proverb for a minute. Take each word and ponder it. Notice how it is saying that we cannot understand someone else fully unless we have lived their life. Empathy is the ability to be able to vicariously live someone else's life so as to understand that person better.

Notice how St. Paul was able to empathize with all people. This was how he was able to bring the Gospel to so many. His saying, that he made himself all things to all people, is another way of saying he tried to walk in their moccasins. Consider the example of St. Francis who broke his own fast and the fast of the brothers out of an act of charity for one of their own members. Notice how gently Francis spoke to the friars as he explained to them the prudence of fasting according to their own bodily needs and not according to some standard set by someone else. Francis could empathize with each of the brothers, and he knew that each one had a different constitution so each one's bodily needs were different. Additionally, he could also empathize with their spiritual desires to become holy by denying themselves. This ability to understand and feel the emotions of his brothers made Francis deeply loved by them.

It is generally easier to empathize with people whose life experiences have been similar to our own. The difficulty with empathy comes when we confront people whose experiences or lifestyles are very different from our own. Yet in order to relate to these people with charity, we need to empathize with them also. By God's grace, St. Francis and St. Paul were able to do this. One way to begin is to ask ourselves a series of questions First, take an outward view: How is that person currently living? What are they currently viewing or reading? Who are their friends? What might their goals in life be? Second, take an inward view: If this were our background, what would we be interested in? What would we want to do? What would our goals be? What would our philosophy of life be? Can we empathize better now, having answered these questions?

Spend a minimum of five minutes meditating on the Virtue of Empathy. Do not write anything during this time. Merely begin your time by praying, "Lord, help me to understand the Virtue of Empathy and how I can empathize more completely with others."

At the end of your meditation time, ask yourself:

Am I able to empathize with anyone? If so, who? If I am not good at empathizing, what can I do to develop this virtue? Think of someone who you do not understand or who irritates you. Using the above questions, try to understand the past life and the present concerns of this individual. Can you empathize a bit better now? How can empathizing with others make me a better person? How can it help me in my spiritual development? How can it help me be a witness for Christ?

Find another section in Scripture which illustrates the Virtue of Empathy. Find a statement of Jesus or an incident in His life that deals with the Virtue of Empathy. Write these into your journal.

If you are a member of a Religious Order, find one place in your Rule or Constitutions which calls for the Virtue of Empathy. Explain why you chose this section.

Practice the Virtue of Empathy this week. Try to empathize with everyone to some degree, but with one person in particular. If it is possible to speak to that person, engage him or her in a conversation which could help you to empathize more closely with that person. You might ask them, for example, how they are doing or how their family is doing. You might pay them a compliment and gauge their response. You might sit by them at lunchtime and casually chat with them. Be conscious of being empathetic. Do you think you have been successful? How does empathy change your attitude toward this individual? Record in your journal any memorable insights or happenings.

Each evening, examine the day for the opportunities you had to practice empathy. Pray, "Lord, help me to empathize with those whom I meet. Let me feel their pain and their joy. May my empathy enable me to respond better to others with Christian love. Amen."

At the end of the week, record in your journal what you have learned from this exercise.

CHAPTER 9

Encouragement

Scripture

Let us hold fast the confession of our hope without wavering, for he who promised is faithful. And let us consider how to stir up one another to love and good works, not neglecting to meet together, as is the habit of some, but encouraging one another, and all the more as you see the Day drawing near. (Hebrews 10:23-25)

Writings of Saint Francis

And if you have done this, I wish to know in this way if you love the Lord and me, His servant and yours: that there is not any brother in the world who has sinned-- however much he could have sinned-- who, after he has looked into your eyes, would never depart without your mercy, if he is looking for mercy. And if he were not looking for mercy, you would ask him if he wants mercy. And if he would sin 1000 times before your eyes, love him more than me so that you may draw him to the Lord; and always be merciful with brothers such as these. (A Letter to a Minister)

Incident from the Life of Saint Francis

There was a certain brother named Riccerio, noble by birth but more noble in character, a lover of God and despiser of himself. With a devout spirit he was led wholeheartedly to attain and possess the favor of the blessed father Francis. He was quite fearful that the holy man Francis would detest him for some secret reason and thus he would become a stranger to the gift of his love. That brother, since he was fearful, thought that any person the holy man Francis loved intimately was also worthy to merit divine favor. On the other hand, he judged that someone to whom he did not show himself kindly and pleasant would incur the wrath of the supreme Judge. This brother turned these matters over in his heart; he silently spoke of these matters to himself, but revealed to no one else his secret thoughts.

One day the blessed father was praying in his cell and that brother came to the place disturbed by his usual thoughts. The holy one of God knew both that the brother had come and understood what was twisting in his heart. So the blessed father immediately called him to himself. "Let no temptation disturb you, my son," he said to him, "and do not be troubled by any thought. You are very dear to me and you should know that, among those dearest to me, you are worthy of my love and intimacy. Come to me confidently whenever you want, knowing you are welcome, and, in this intimacy, speak freely." That brother was amazed, and from then on, became even more reverent. The more that he grew in the holy father's grace, the more he began to enjoy God's mercy with confidence. (The Life of Saint Francis by Thomas of Celano, Chapter XVIII)

SAINT FRANCIS SPENT a great deal of time encouraging his friars. They certainly needed encouragement to live their poor and tenuous lives in fraternal love for one another and in total trust on the providence of God. Encouraging his brothers was not an option for Francis. It was a necessity!

How necessary is encouragement for everyone else? Consider a sports team. If you have ever played team sports, you know how cheers and jeers from the grandstand can either encourage or discourage the players. Those who are cheering or jeering understand this effect. That's why they are so loud!

We all recognize that disparaging remarks sting. However, do we ever think that, as we go through life, we are actually jeering someone if we aren't cheering for them? Indifference or lack of response is disheartening even though nothing is said. Here's an example. Let's say that you worked diligently on a project and brought it to your boss who took it, glanced at it, and said, "OK. Put it on my desk. Now the next thing is . . ." Wouldn't you feel slighted, as if your hard work and attention to detail were unappreciated? Would you work just as diligently on the next project?

You can recognize encouraging remarks. "Great job!" "I wish I had your talent!" "Things have to start to look up from here." However, suppose you can't think of a single encouraging remark for someone. Try these examples. "I know you're trying." "Don't give up. You can get it right." "Let's see how we can make the best of this situation." Ask the Holy Spirit to help you say something genuine and truthful that will also give your listener hope. For hope is the result of encouragement.

Finally, remember to encourage yourself. A stream of discouraging thoughts fosters negativity and draws one away from God Who is beauty, truth, hope, and love. God can overcome every situation in His way if we surrender all to Him and trust Him. If you are discouraged, place yourself and your situation into the hands of your heavenly Father. Then encourage yourself with the words, "He takes care of the sparrow. He will take care of me." Believe it because it is true.

Spend a minimum of five minutes meditating on the Virtue of Encouragement. Do not write anything during this time. Merely begin your time by praying, "Lord, help me to understand the Virtue of Encouragement and where I need it in my life. Help me to know how to share a word of encouragement with others."

At the end of your meditation time, ask yourself:

Am I good encourager? Do I see encouragement as a virtue? Do I think encouragement is important? Who in my life needs encouragement? How can I encourage them? How can I encourage myself?

Find another section in Scripture which illustrates the Virtue of Encouragement. Find a statement of Jesus or an incident in His life that deals with the Virtue of Encouragement. Write these into your journal.

If you are a member of a Religious Order, find one place in your Rule or Constitutions which calls for the Virtue of Encouragement. Explain why you chose this section.

Practice the Virtue of Encouragement this week by encouraging yourself and at least one other person each day. Record in your journal any memorable insights or happenings.

Each evening, examine your day for the times when you were encouraging and for the times when you could have encouraged someone but didn't. Pray each night, "Lord, help me to become an encouraging person. Enable me to be attentive to opportunities where an encouraging word will make a difference. You encourage me in my spiritual journey. Help me to encourage others on theirs. Amen."

At the end of the week, record in your journal what you have learned from this exercise.

CHAPTER 10

Eucharistic Reverence

Scripture

While they were eating, Jesus took bread, said the blessing, broke it, and giving it to his disciples said, "Take and eat; this is my body." Then he took a cup, gave thanks, and gave it to them, saying, "Drink from it, all of you, for this is my blood of the covenant, which will be shed on behalf of many for the forgiveness of sins. I tell you, from now on I shall not drink this fruit of the vine until the day when I drink it with you new in the kingdom of my Father." (Matthew 26:26-29)

Writings of Saint Francis

Behold daily He humbles Himself as when from His "royal throne" He came into the womb of the Virgin; daily He Himself comes to us with like humility; daily He descends from the bosom of His Father upon the altar in the hands of the priest. And as He appeared in true flesh to the Holy Apostles, so now He shows Himself to us in the sacred Bread; and as they by means of their fleshly eyes saw only His flesh, yet contemplating Him with their spiritual eyes, believed Him to be God, so we, seeing bread and wine with bodily eyes, see and firmly believe it to be His most holy Body and true and living Blood. And in this way our Lord is ever with His faithful, as He Himself says: "Behold I am with you all days, even to the consummation of the world." (Admonitions 1)

Incident from the Life of Saint Francis

Saint Francis wrote the following letter to the clergy, asking that his friars distribute it to all the clergy. This was probably written after the Fourth Lateran Council at which the Pope first described the abuses regarding the Eucharist and then called for reverence for the Body of Christ. Francis, who was present at this Council, took these words to heart, as evidenced in this Letter.

Let us all consider, O clerics, the great sin and ignorance of which some are guilty regarding the most holy Body and Blood of our Lord Jesus Christ and His most holy Name and the written words of consecration. For we know that the Body cannot exist until after these words of consecration. For we have nothing and we see nothing of the Most High Himself in this world except [His] Body and Blood, names and words by which we have been created and redeemed from death to life.

But let all those who administer such most holy mysteries, especially those who do so indifferently, consider among themselves how poor the chalices, corporals, and linens may be where the Body and Blood of our Lord Jesus Christ is sacrificed. And by many It is left in wretched places and carried by the way disrespectfully, received unworthily and administered to others indiscriminately. Again His Names and written words are sometimes trampled underfoot, for the sensual man perceiveth not these things that are of God. Shall we not by all these things be moved with a sense of duty when the good Lord Himself places Himself in our hands and we handle Him and receive Him daily? Are we unmindful that we must needs fall into His hands?

Let us then at once and resolutely correct these faults and others; and wheresoever the most holy Body of our Lord Jesus Christ may be improperly reserved and abandoned, let It be removed thence and let It be put and enclosed in a precious place. In like manner wheresoever the Names and written words of the Lord may be found in unclean places they ought to be collected and put away in a decent place. And we know that we are bound above all to observe all these things by the commandments of the Lord and the constitutions of holy Mother Church. And let him who does not act thus know that he shall have to render an account therefor before our Lord Jesus Christ on the day of judgment. And let him who may cause copies of this writing to be made, to the end that it may be the better observed, know that he is blessed by the Lord. (Letter to All the Clergy)

READ AGAIN SAINT Francis's words on the Blessed Sacrament. While most people think of Saint Francis as the bird bath saint, they have widely missed the mark.

Saint Francis should be pictured with a chalice. He was deeply devoted to the Eucharist. The passages above are a mere fraction of Francis's writings on the Eucharist.

Why is the Eucharist so important? It is important because the Eucharist is the Lord Jesus Christ physically present among us. Albeit, He is present humbly, under the appearance of defenseless, simple bread. Devotion to the Eucharist is a virtue because it recognizes that our great, eternal, uncreated God submits Himself to us in this unassuming way. What does this teach us about how we should act?

We can begin by analyzing how we prepare to receive the Eucharist. Do we ask God to fill us with Himself? Do we meditate on the great gift of grace that God is giving us? Do we walk reverently forward and show a sign of respect to the Lord whom we are going to take into our body? After receiving, do we communicate in prayer with God, Who is now physically within us? Do we understand what that means for us and for everyone else who has also received Him?

Spend a minimum of five minutes meditating on the Virtue of Eucharistic Reverence. Do not write anything during this time. Merely begin your time by praying, "Lord, I am a weak creature who cannot comprehend the ineffable mystery of love in the Eucharist. Help me to understand the Virtue of Eucharistic Reverence. Help me to give suitable honor to our Lord's Body and Blood. Amen."

At the end of your meditation time, ask yourself:

Do I believe in the Real Presence of our Lord in the Blessed Sacrament? If not, how can I resolve my disbelief? Am I reverent to the Blessed Sacrament? How can I foster and deepen this reverence? How can my behavior and my words foster reverence in others? How can I help others to understand the Real Presence?

Find another section in Scripture which illustrates the Virtue of Eucharistic Reverence. Find a statement of Jesus or an incident in His life that deals with the Virtue of Eucharistic Reverence. Write these into your journal.

If you are a member of a Religious Order, find one place in your Rule or Constitutions which calls for the Virtue of Eucharistic Reverence. Explain why you chose this section.

Practice the Virtue of Eucharistic Reverence this week. If you cannot receive the Blessed Sacrament, make a Spiritual Communion. Pray, *"My Jesus, I believe that You are present in the Most Holy Sacrament. I love You above all things, and I desire to receive You into my soul. Since I cannot at this moment receive You sacramentally, come at least spiritually into my heart. I embrace You as if You were already there and unite myself wholly to You. Never permit me to be separated from You. Amen."* You may also consider obtaining the Chaplet of Adoration (Available from the Confraternity of Penitents Holy Angels Gift Shop, cfpholyangels.com) which can be used to adore the Blessed Sacrament anywhere, or you might adore the Blessed Sacrament through internet adoration sites. Searching the world wide web will reveal several websites. Record in your journal any memorable insights or happenings.

Each evening review the times during which you showed reverence to the Eucharist. If you have not done well, resolve to improve. Pray each night, "Lord, help me to treat Your Body and Blood with the reverence deserving of You. I am weak and easily distracted. Help me to focus on Your Presence as You are focused on me. Amen."

At the end of the week, record in your journal what you have learned from this exercise.

CHAPTER 11

Evangelization

Scripture

And he said to them, "Go into all the world and preach the gospel to all creation." (Mark 16:15)

Writings of Saint Francis

In the Name of the Father and of the Son and of the Holy Ghost. Amen. All to whom this letter may come, I, Brother Francis, your little servant, pray and conjure you by the charity which God is, and with the will to kiss your feet, to receive these balm-bearing words of our Lord Jesus Christ with humility and charity and to put them in practice kindly and to observe them perfectly. And let those who do not know how to read have them read often and let them keep them by them with holy operation unto the end, for they are spirit and life. And those who do not do this shall render an account on the day of Judgment before the tribunal of Christ. And all those who shall receive them kindly and understand them and send them to others as example, if they persevere in them unto the end, may the Father and the Son and the Holy Ghost bless them. Amen. (First Version of the Letter to the Faithful)

Incident from the Life of Saint Francis

While many were joining the brothers, as already related, the blessed father Francis was traveling through the Spoleto Valley. He reached a place near Bevagna, in which a great multitude of birds of different types gathered, including doves, crows, and others commonly called monaclae. When Francis, the most blessed servant of God, saw them, he ran swiftly toward them, leaving his companions on the road. He was a man of great fervor, feeling much sweetness and tenderness even toward lesser, irrational creatures. When he was already very close, seeing that they awaited him, he greeted them in his usual way. He was quite surprised, however, because the birds did not take flight, as they usually do. Filled with great joy, he humbly requested that they listen to the word of God. . . .

After the birds had listened so reverently to the word of God, he began to accuse himself of negligence because he had not preached to them before. From that day on, he carefully exhorted all birds, all animals, all reptiles, and also all insensible creatures to praise and love the Creator, because daily, invoking the name of the Savior, he observed their obedience in his own experience. . . .

At the time the venerable father Francis preached to the birds, as reported above, he went around the towns and villages, sowing the seed of divine blessings everywhere, until he reached the city of Ascoli. There he spoke the word of God with his usual fervor. By a change of the right hand of the Most High, nearly all the people were filled with such grace and devotion that they were trampling each other in their eagerness to hear and see him. Thirty men, cleric and lay, at that time received the habit of holy religion from him. (Thomas of Celano, The Life of Saint Francis, Chapters XXI and XXII)

IN A WORLD very much attuned to political correctness and tolerance, we may feel that it's prudent to keep our faith to ourselves. This was not the message of Jesus! It certainly was not the mind of Francis who preached the gospel not only to people but also to "all creation." Do you believe that Jesus is the Son of God? If not, then why do you profess to be a Christian? If you do believe that He is the Son of God, how can you pick and choose which of His directives to follow?

Jesus did not make evangelization an option or the prerogative of the apostles and disciples only. Anyone who follows Christ is called to "preach the gospel to all creation." Why would you hold back a message of hope and love? Only fear can keep a believer in Christ from proclaiming Him loud and clear.

Evangelization is a virtue that relies upon a great many other virtues for its success. Those who practice the Virtue of Evangelization will necessarily practice attentiveness, enthusiasm, faith, and charity. If they don't practice these virtues, their Evangelization will not draw people to Christ but will, instead, be counter-productive and turn them away from the Lord.

Evangelization means sharing the gospel with others. While it does not mean being intolerant of their faith or lack thereof, it does mean sharing the GOOD news. You never know what someone needs to hear. If you feel the Holy Spirit prompting you to be a witness to the Lord, by all means follow the inspiration.

Evangelization involves more than witnessing to Christ. It also involves timing. Perhaps you want to share Jesus's message with someone, but you feel a block against doing so. If this block feels like it's outside of you, like an invisible hand stopping you from going forward, consider that it might be the prompting of the Holy Spirit. Generally, those thoughts that come from within – fears, justifications, and doubts – are simply prompted by fear and should be prayerfully brought to God. So, why would the Holy Spirit not want you to share the gospel? The answer lies in God's timing.

You know that, if you want to have fresh tomatoes in your garden, you need to plant some tomato plants. However, tomato plants need to be placed in the ground in late spring after all danger of frost is past. Moreover, you need to fork the soil and add nutrients that help tomatoes grow before you plant them. Once planted, you need to keep them weeded and watered. If you plant tomatoes in September in Minnesota, you will definitely not get any tomatoes from them because the frost will kill the plants before any fruit is ready. Further, if you plant tomatoes in Minnesota in late spring, but don't prepare the soil or tend the plants, you won't get many tomatoes, if any. Evangelization is like planting tomato plants. The time for planting has to be right, and you need to prepare the soil before planting and then tend the plants afterwards.

How do you evangelize if the Holy Spirit seems to be saying, "Not now?" Follow that prompting of the Holy Spirit and share the message but without using the name of Christ. For example, instead of saying, "Jesus loves you," say, "You know, you are loveable." The person may not be ready yet to hear the name of Christ, but may be ready to accept that he or she can be loved with no strings attached. You have just prepared the person's heart to receive, at some future time, the deeper message, "Jesus loves you."

Spend a minimum of five minutes meditating on the Virtue of Evangelization. Do not write anything during this time. Merely begin your time by praying, "Lord, help me to understand the Virtue of Evangelization and how I need to implement this virtue in my life."

At the end of your meditation time, ask yourself: Do I evangelize? Why or why not? Be honest with your answer. What does your answer tell you about yourself? What do you need to work on regarding your obligation as a Christian to be an evangelist?

Find another section in Scripture which illustrates the Virtue of Evangelization. Find a statement of Jesus or an incident in His life that deals with the Virtue of Evangelization. Write these into your journal.

If you are a member of a Religious Order, find one place in your Rule or Constitutions which calls for the Virtue of Evangelization. Explain why you chose this section.

Practice the Virtue of Evangelization this week. Who needs to know about God's love? How can you tell them? When you do, that is evangelization. Record in your journal any memorable insights or happenings.

Each evening, examine your day for the times when you were able to practice evangelization and for the times when you could have evangelized but did not. Pray each night, "Lord, make me receptive to the Holy Spirit, so that I can recognize opportunities to evangelize. Give me the courage, at those moments of recognition, to make Your love known. I am often a coward, Lord. Make me a bolder proclaimer of Your message. I put myself at Your disposal for this obligation. Amen."

At the end of the week, record in your journal what you have learned from this exercise.

Chapter 12

Example

Scripture

"If I then, the Lord and the Teacher, washed your feet, you also ought to wash one another's feet. For I gave you an example that you also should do as I did to you. Truly, truly, I say to you, a slave is not greater than his master, nor is one who is sent greater than the one who sent him." (John 13:14-16)

Writings of Saint Francis

And let the ministers and servants remember that the Lord says: I have not "come to be ministered unto, but to minister," and that to them is committed the care of the souls of their brothers, of whom, if any should be lost through their fault and bad example, they will have to give an account before the Lord Jesus Christ in the day of judgment. (First Rule, Chapter IV)

Incident from the Life of Saint Francis

Thus one time in winter, one of the companions, who was his guardian, acquired a piece of fox fur because of the illness of the spleen and the cold of his stomach. He asked him to permit him to have it sewn under his tunic next to his stomach and spleen, especially because it was then extremely cold. But from the moment he began to serve Christ until the day of his death, in any weather, he did not want to wear or have anything but a single patched tunic.

Blessed Francis answered him: "If you want me to wear that fur under the tunic, allow me to sew a piece of the fur on the outside of my tunic as an indication to people that I have a piece of fur underneath." And this is what he had done; and, although it was a necessity on account of his illnesses, he did not wear it long. (The Assisi Compilation, Section 81)

JESUS TOLD HIS apostles to do as He had done. He emphasized this many times. We are to follow His example, even to the point of taking up our own crosses, following in Christ's footsteps, and dying to self to live for Him. Saint Francis took this instruction to heart. He tried to live his life imitating Christ. He took very seriously the popular motto "what would Jesus do?"

What would Jesus do? If we try to do what Jesus would do, we will automatically become a good example to others. Why is being a good example a virtue? When we do good, we portray Christ to the world by how we act and what we say. The familiar saying, "You are the only gospel some people will ever read" holds true, sadly, for many people who will learn about Jesus solely by how Christians portray Him and live for Him.

Never underestimate the virtue of example. Children do what their peers do. Teens talk like their friends. Employees imitate each other's work habits. How many times have you seen a prayerful person at church and suddenly your church posture became more prayerful, too? We may not realize that we are being an example to others, but perhaps we ought to think of that. Saint Francis thought of it constantly. He never wanted to give bad example, nor did he want to portray himself as someone he was not. He wanted to be a genuine follower of Christ, because he knew that his example was a means of spreading the gospel. People learned about Jesus just by seeing Francis. What are people learning about Jesus by seeing you?

Spend a minimum of five minutes meditating on the Virtue of Example. Do not write anything during this time. Merely begin your time by praying, "Lord, help me to be a good example to others. When they see or hear me, they must think of You. Help me to recognize where I am giving good example and where I am not. Give me the courage to do better."

At the end of your meditation time, ask yourself: When is it easy for me to be a good example? When is it difficult? What causes me to fail in being a good example? Do I want to be a good example? Why or why not? Should I want to be a good example? Why or why not?

Find another section in Scripture which illustrates the Virtue of Example. Find a statement of Jesus or an incident in His life that deals with the Virtue of Example. Write these into your journal.

If you are a member of a Religious Order, find one place in your Rule or Constitutions which calls for the Virtue of Example. Explain why you chose this section.

Practice the Virtue of Example this week. Record in your journal any memorable insights or happenings.

Each evening, examine your day for the times when you were or were not a good example to others. What caused you to be an example? What caused the example to be good or poor? Where could you have been an example and you preferred to remain incognito? Evaluate each day in light of your example to others. Pray each night, "Lord, grant me the grace, the perseverance, and the courage to always be a good example to others. Amen."

At the end of the week, record in your journal what you have learned from this exercise.

CHAPTER 13

Faith

Scripture
And He said to them, "Why are you afraid? Do you still have no faith?" (Mark 4:40)

Writings of Saint Francis
And the Lord gave me so much faith in churches that I would simply pray and say thus: "We adore Thee Lord Jesus Christ here 1 and in all Thy churches which are in the whole world, and we bless Thee because by Thy holy cross Thou hast redeemed the world." (St. Francis of Assisi, Testament)

Incident from the Life of Saint Francis
The man of God, who was already holy because of his holy intention, was accustomed to enter the cave, while his companion waited outside, and inspired by a new and extraordinary spirit he would pray to his Father in secret. He acted in such a way that no one would know what was happening within. Wisely taking the occasion of the good to conceal the better, he consulted God alone about his holy purpose. He prayed with all his heart that the eternal and true God guide his way and teach him to do His will. (The Life of Saint Francis by Thomas of Celano, Chapter III)

WHEN ST. FRANCIS was undergoing his conversion process and discerning the way God wanted him to go, he took a friend along with him. While the friend waited outside, Francis went into a cave to pray alone to God. He took to heart the Scripture verse that tells us to pray in secret. Yet, in order to pray, we must have faith. St. Francis became discouraged at different times of his life, but his faith in God did not waver. Through his conversion, he learned to transfer his faith in himself or in others to God alone. When he did this, he was free to have nothing, to expect no privileges, and to live in the present moment.

Faith is the virtue that tells us that a Benevolent Power is in charge of the world. Moreover, this Power is concerned with us. This Power created us, not as toys or objects of art, but as sons and daughters. We call this Power God, but John the Evangelist gave the name Love to this eternal being. Faith is the virtue that causes us to look to this Power, whom we call God, instead of to ourselves or to others. We believe that Infinite Wisdom knows more than our fragile knowledge, and that Divine Power can work in ways our limited human abilities cannot comprehend. Moreover, because God is good, He makes all things work for our ultimate salvation.

We cannot see God. Through the virtue of faith, we believe by seeking out the effects of God. Although Jesus is God made flesh, an image of God graciously granted that we might ponder Him, He cannot be put under a microscope and analyzed as we might a human cell. We learn about Christ through the Gospels, but our direct experience of Him through the Eucharist requires faith to believe in His Presence. Through the virtue of Faith, we experience God through His actions upon creation. Just as the invisible wind keeps a kite in the air, the invisible God maintains the order of creation. We cannot see the wind, but we know it exists, because the kite flies. We cannot see God, but we know He exists, because there is order in creation.

Nearly everyone undergoes a test of faith at least once in a lifetime. Sometimes God seems absent, or He appears to act too slowly or indifferently. God may even seem cruel or unfeeling. At these times we may cling to our faith with our fingernails, because we choose to believe. Faith comes down to one reality: if there is no God and we have believed there is God, when we die we will have lost nothing, because we will be nothing, However, if there is a God and we do not believe, we shall spend eternity missing the heaven God promised to the faithful. When one weighs the one hundred years of a lifetime (and that would be excessive) against the eons of eternity, the choice to believe becomes completely prudent.

Spend a minimum of five minutes meditating on the Virtue of Faith. Do not write anything during this time. Merely begin your time by praying, "Lord, increase my faith. Help me to understand why Faith is a virtue and how I may prepare my heart for a deeper Faith."

At the end of your meditation time, ask yourself:

What is faith? What do I believe? Do I have faith? How strong is my faith? Where is my faith strongest? Where is my faith weak? Can my faith be stronger? Should I ask God for an increase of faith? Am I afraid to do that? Why or why not?

Find another section in Scripture which illustrates the Virtue of Faith. Find a statement of Jesus or an incident in His life that deals with the Virtue of Faith. Write these into your journal.

If you are a member of a Religious Order, find one place in your Rule or Constitutions which calls for the Virtue of Faith. Explain why you chose this section.

Practice the Virtue of Faith this week by continually turning over to God's Providence all your cares and plans. Record in your journal any memorable insights or happenings.

Each evening, examine your day for the times when you called upon or recognized your faith and for the times when you looked everywhere but to God for guidance. Pray each night, "Lord, I believe, but help my unbelief. Strengthen my faith so that, in every difficulty, I look first to You. Deepen my faith so that, in every joy, I praise You. Broaden my faith so that in every confusion I seek Your clarity. Amen."

At the end of the week, record in your journal what you have learned from this exercise.

Chapter 14

Fraternity

Scripture

We love because he first loved us. Those who say, 'I love God', and hate their brothers or sisters, are liars; for those who do not love a brother or sister whom they have seen, cannot love God whom they have not seen. The commandment we have from him is this: those who love God must love their brothers and sisters also. (1 John 4:19-21)

Writings of Saint Francis

And let all the brothers, the ministers and servants as well as the others, take care not to be troubled or angered because of the fault or bad example of another, for the devil desires to corrupt many through the sin of one; but let them spiritually help him who has sinned, as best they can; for he that is whole needs not a physician, but he that is sick. In like manner let not all the brothers have power and authority, especially among themselves, for as the Lord says in the Gospel: "The princes of the Gentiles lord it over them: and they that are the greater exercise power upon them." It shall not be thus among the brothers, but whosoever will be the greater among them, let him be their minister and servant, and he that is the greater among them let him be as the younger, and he who is the first, let him be as the last. Let not any brother do evil or speak evil to another; let them rather in the spirit of charity willingly serve and obey each other: and this is the true and holy obedience of our Lord Jesus Christ. (Earlier Rule, Section V)

Incident from the Life of Saint Francis

They loved one another from the heart and each one served and took care of the other, as a mother serves and cares for her son. The fire of love burned so intensely in them, that they would have willingly sacrificed their lives not only for the name of our Lord Jesus Christ but also for one another.

One day, two brothers were walking along the road when suddenly a simpleton began throwing stones at them. One of them, seeing that a stone was about to strike his brother, ran directly in front of him. Because of ardent mutual love, he preferred that the stone strike him rather than his brother. They frequently did these and similar things. (The Anonymous of Perugia, Chapter VI)

FRATERNITY MEANS BROTHERHOOD, but by extension, it also means sisterhood. A college fraternity or sorority is intended to be a group of people who live together and treat each other as family. Many times college groups fall far short of the goal. However, St. Francis wanted his brothers to be a true fraternity. St. Clare wanted her sisters to be a true sorority. Thus, the early penitents met monthly to become a true family in the church.

St. John the evangelist tells us that our fraternity extends not only to those we know, not only to those who agree with us, not only to those who believe in Jesus, but also to the whole world. If we do not love others whom God has made, how can we love God? This love of others creates a fraternity of human beings in which all are brothers and sisters. This incident regarding the brothers who followed St. Francis shows the fraternal love among the early brothers. Francis, in his writings, takes for granted that those who follow him will be brothers. The writing in this reflection is one example of the many that Francis used to exhort his brothers to understand their fraternity and to show fraternal love.

Fraternity is not often thought of as a virtue, yet it most surely is one, because fraternity is a mindset that treats each individual with respect, dignity, and love. How would the world look different to us if we saw everyone as our brother or sister? Do you have a brother or sister? Have you had a good relationship with him or her? If you have, thank God for that. If you have not had a good relationship, now is the time to see if the walls can be broken down and the relationships mended. Forgiving perceived wrongs is a part of the virtue of Fraternity, because it is difficult to see the whole world as our family of brothers and sisters if we are estranged from our own blood brother or sister. Fraternity means loving and treating others as part of our family. When we begin to see others as brothers and sisters, we develop a special love and care for them that mirrors that of the good Samaritan. By tending to the stranger, whom he saw as his neighbor or brother, beaten by robbers at the roadside, Jesus, through this parable, shows us that it is possible to love someone without knowing them.

Spend a minimum of five minutes meditating on the Virtue of Fraternity. Do not write anything during this time. Merely begin your time by praying, "Lord, I do not fully understand the virtue of Fraternity. Help me to see where I am lacking Fraternity in my life. Open my eyes to others as my brothers and sisters in the human race, and to Christians as my brothers and sisters in Jesus. Give me a fraternal love for all people, for You made each person in Your image. Please remove any blocks against my seeing life through a fraternal lens."

At the end of your meditation time, ask yourself:

What is my idea of fraternity? Do I see all people as my brothers and sisters? Why or why not? What is blocking my sense of fraternity against others? Can I feel a fraternity with my enemy or with enemies of the faith? Why would God want us to see all people not only as part of the human family but also as part of my OWN family? How do I actually treat my own family members? Is it more difficult to feel fraternity with them than with distant people whom I meet only in my imagination? Do I desire the Virtue of Fraternity? If not, why not?

Find another section in Scripture which illustrates the Virtue of Fraternity. Find a statement of Jesus or an incident in His life that deals with the Virtue of Fraternity. Write these into your journal.

If you are a member of a Religious Order, find one place in your Rule or Constitutions which calls for the Virtue of Fraternity. Explain why you chose this section.

Practice the Virtue of Fraternity this week by continually trying to see all people as your brothers and sisters and by trying to treat them with fraternal love and respect. Record in your journal any memorable insights or happenings.

Each evening, examine your day for the times when you recognized someone else as a brother or sister. Did you show fraternal love to that person? If not, how could you have done so? Pray each night, "Lord, I know I am Your child. I know that You created me and every other human being as well. Therefore, I know logically that we are all brothers and sisters as we are children of the same Father. Still, I have difficulty living the Virtue of Fraternity in my life. Open my mind and my heart to love others as my brothers and sisters. I pray for a deeper love. Amen

At the end of the week, record in your journal what you have learned from this exercise.

CHAPTER 15

Generosity

Scripture

"If anyone wants to sue you and take your shirt, let him have your coat also. Whoever forces you to go one mile, go with him two. Give to him who asks of you, and do not turn away from him who wants to borrow from you. (Matthew 5:40-42)

Writings of Saint Francis

Blessed is the servant who gives up all his goods to the Lord God, for he who retains anything for himself hides "his Lord's money," and that "which he thinketh he hath shall be taken away from him." (Admonitions 19)

Incident from the Life of Saint Francis

In Celano at winter time, Saint Francis was wearing a piece of folded cloth as a cloak, which a man from Tivoli, a friend of the brothers, had lent him. While he was at the palace of the bishop of the Marsi, an old woman came up to him, begging for alms. He quickly unfastened the cloth from his neck, and, although it belonged to someone else, he gave it to the poor old woman, saying: "go and make yourself a tunic; you really need it." The old woman laughed; she was stunned-- I do not know if it was out of fear or joy-- and took the piece of cloth from his hands. She ran off quickly, so that delay might not bring the danger of having to give it back, and cut it with scissors. But when she saw that the cut cloth would not be enough for a tunic, she returned to the saint, knowing his earlier kindness, and showed him that the material was not enough. The saint turned his eyes on his companion, who had just the same cloth covering his back. "Brother," he said, "do you hear what this old woman is saying? For the love of God, let us bear with the cold! Give the poor woman the cloth so she can finish her tunic."

He gave his, the companion offered his as well, and both left naked so the old woman could be clothed. (The Remembrance of the Desire of a Soul by Thomas of Celano, Chapter LIII)

GENEROSITY IS MORE than giving. It means giving from your want, from your need, not just giving what you have left over. Can you remember a time when someone showed you generosity? Perhaps you received a material object or financial help. Additionally, generosity can be shown with the gift of time or a listening ear. We can be generous in sharing our talents or our knowledge. Generosity is giving an undeserved gift without expecting gratitude or repayment. Generosity is casting your bread upon the water and not expecting it to return.

The incident of Saint Francis giving away his cloak is typical of Francis. He gave away many things to anyone in need. People sometimes say others are generous to a fault. If that is possible, it would describe St. Francis. Yet, is it possible to be generous to a fault? Francis would not think so. He would consider how generous God is with us. He gives us His very best. He gives us Himself in His Son. He gives us the Holy Spirit to be with us always. He gives us the miracle of His Son truly present in every celebration of the Eucharist. He gives us who believe and who follow Him the gift of eternal life. We can never out give God. Francis thanked God profusely and constantly for His generosity. Have you thanked God today?

How can you practice generosity? How about giving someone else the larger portion, letting someone take your place in line, giving a chatty talker a listening ear, buttoning your lip so as not to undermine someone else's overblown tale? How can we be generous with God? The Israelites had written into their law that the first born of the flock, the very best issue, was to be sacrificed to the Lord. Generosity was enforced by decree. Jesus is not so legalistic with us. Yet shouldn't we still give God the best and finest and first of our produce, our talents, our time? Are you courageous enough to ask God how to be generous?

Spend a minimum of five minutes meditating on the Virtue of Generosity. Do not write anything during this time. Merely begin your time by praying,

"Generous and gracious Lord, You have given much to me who deserves so little. Help me to understand the Virtue of Generosity and where I need it in my life."

At the end of your meditation time, ask yourself:

Am I a generous person? How do I show generosity? How do I miss showing generosity? Do I recognize the generous responses of others toward me? Do I know any generous people? What is my attitude toward them? What am I most generous with? What am I most stingy with? Does my generosity need a boost? How can I become a more generous person?

Find another section in Scripture which illustrates the Virtue of Generosity. Find a statement of Jesus or an incident in His life that deals with the Virtue of Generosity. Write these into your journal.

If you are a member of a Religious Order, find one place in your Rule or Constitutions which calls for the Virtue of Generosity. Explain why you chose this section.

Practice the Virtue of Generosity this week. Record in your journal any memorable insights or happenings.

Each evening, examine the day for the opportunities you had to show generosity. Pray, "Lord, I want to be generous with my time, love, money, and possessions. I know that many times I hold back when I can give. Lord, help me to trust that, when I give of myself, I will be filled and not depleted. Help me to trust that the more I give of myself, the more of who I am will become clear to me. Guide me to know what to give, when to give, to whom to give, and how to give. Lord, You are the Generous Giver. Help me in my weakness to imitate You. Amen."

At the end of the week, record in your journal what you have learned from this exercise.

CHAPTER 16

Gratitude

Scripture
In everything give thanks: for this is the will of God in Christ Jesus concerning you.
(1 Thessalonians 5:18)

Writings of Saint Francis
And I ask the sick brother that he give thanks to the Creator for all things, and that
he desire to be as God wills him to be, whether sick or well; for all whom the Lord has
predestined to eternal life are disciplined by the rod of afflictions and infirmities, and
the spirit of compunction; as the Lord says: "Such as I love I rebuke and chastise."
(First Rule, Chapter X)

Incident from the Life of Saint Francis
Then the blessed Francis called them all to himself and told them many things about
the kingdom of God, contempt of the world, denial of their own will, and subjection of
the body. He separated them into four groups of two each.

"Go, my dear brothers," he said to them, "two by two through different parts of
the world, announcing peace to the people and penance for the remission of sins. Be
patient in trials, confident that the Lord will fulfill His plan and promise. Respond
humbly to those who question you. Bless those who persecute you. Give thanks to
those who harm you and bring false charges against you, for because of these things an
eternal kingdom is prepared for us." . . .

Only a short time had passed when St. Francis began desiring to see them all. He prayed to the Lord, who gathered the dispersed of Israel, mercifully to bring them together soon. So it happened in a short time: they came together at the same time according to his desire, without any human summons, giving thanks to God. (The Life of Saint Francis by Thomas of Celano, Chapter XII)

How CAN YOU tell if you have a grateful heart? A grateful heart is one that gives thanks to God in all circumstances. Can you say that you have a grateful heart? If not, how can you develop one?

A grateful heart begins by recognizing that God is in charge of our life. Everything that happens to us comes from His active or permissive Will. Nothing that occurs to us or to anyone else is outside the active or permissive Will of God. A grateful heart does not mean that we thank God for the hurt, the pain, the disease, or the disaster that has befallen us or someone else. It does mean that we thank God for what He will work through this pain, this disease, this disaster, or this hurt. Sometimes, the only way to learn what God wishes to teach us is through the acceptance of pain.

Think of a child who wants one toy and then another and then another and then another and then another. If the parent continues to give the child every toy that the child requests, the child will form the impression that every desire is fulfilled. On the other hand, a wise parent will deny a child's request on occasion, in order to teach the child a valuable lesson. It's at these times that the reason for the denial of a toy is not that the parent lacks the money to pay for it. Instead, the parent wishes to teach the lesson that not every desire comes to pass. This hard lesson may cause a temper tantrum or raise an outcry of unfair. However, the earlier this lesson is learned, the better it is for the child's emotional health. For example, imagine a child. Let's call him Jack. Jack grows up, receiving everything that he requests. So, when he applies for college he assumes he'll get in. However, when he finds out that his request for admittance is denied, he becomes angry and irrational. As a result of his upbringing, Jack has great difficulty dealing with this denial. He may try to force the college to accept him. He may grow depressed. He may even question the meaning of his continued existence. Had Jack's parents refused him a request here and there as a child, he may have been better prepared to face this college rejection with greater strength of spirit.

When we have a grateful heart, we give thanks to God for whatever is happening in our lives because we know that God is at work. We know that God does not have to give us everything that we want, but that He will give us what we need. He knows our needs better than we do. God's sole goal is to make us happy in the next world with Him. He achieves this through the purification of our faults. He allows us to feel miserable at times, not receiving what we desire, so that we can realize that everything here on earth is fleeting. This includes our wealth, our health, our friends, our family, our intelligence, our good looks, our possessions, our ideas, our reputation, and anything else we hold highly and often above our love of God. All must be held loosely, nothing taken for granted.

The stories of St. Francis are replete with times when he was grateful to God in very difficult circumstances. They tell of his praising God for being insulted, for being ill, for being misunderstood. At the time of his greatest trial, when he was blind and ill at San Damiano, Francis wrote his greatest prayer of praise, the Canticle of the Creatures. He was grateful because he knew that everything he had value was nothing compared to the value of eternal life. He realized that God had saved him from a worldly life to prepare him for that eternal life, an eternity with God in all His Glory.

Spend a minimum of five minutes meditating on the Virtue of Gratitude. Do not write anything during this time. Merely begin your time by praying, "Lord, help me to develop a grateful heart." Then think of something in your life that you find difficult to be thankful for. Pray: "Lord, this is happening in my life. My heart is anything but grateful regarding it. Open my eyes to see Your hand at work here. Open my heart to believe that You will bring graces out of this trial." Then listen to what God wishes to say.

At the end of your meditation time, ask yourself:

What am I grateful for? What am I not grateful for? What is causing me anger or bitterness or grief in my life right now? What can I be grateful about in these circumstances? When trials come, what can I do to be thankful to God?

Find another section in Scripture which illustrates the Virtue of Gratitude. Find a statement of Jesus or an incident in His life that deals with the Virtue of Gratitude. Write these into your journal.

If you are a member of a Religious Order, find one place in your Rule or Constitutions which calls for the Virtue of Gratitude. Explain why you chose this section.

Practice the Virtue of Gratitude this week. Record in your journal any memorable insights or happenings.

Each evening, examine your day for the times when you were grateful to God and for the times when you lacked gratitude. Pray each night, "Lord, turn my ungrateful heart into a grateful one. Help me to trust in Your wisdom and power at work in my life, even in the things that trouble me or frustrate my plans. You have promised me eternal life. You have given me life in this world to prepare me for life in the next. How can I not be grateful for these gifts? Make my heart more grateful to You. Amen."

At the end of the week, record in your journal what you have learned from this exercise.

CHAPTER 17

Honesty

Scripture
Lying lips are an abomination to the Lord, but those who act faithfully are his delight.
(Proverbs 12:22)

Writings of Saint Francis
And let one make known clearly his wants to another, in order that he may find and receive what are necessary for him. And let everyone love and nourish his brother as a mother loves and nourishes her son, in so far as God gives them grace. (First Rule, Chapter IX)

Incident from the Life of Saint Francis
Thus one time in winter, one of the companions, who was his guardian, acquired a piece of fox fur because of the illness of the spleen and the cold of his stomach. He asked him to permit him to have it sewn under his tunic next to his stomach and spleen, especially because it was then extremely cold. But from the moment he began to serve Christ until the day of his death, in any weather, he did not want to wear or have anything but a single patched tunic.

Blessed Francis answered him: "If you want me to wear that fur under the tunic, allow me to sew a piece of fur on the outside of my tunic as an indication to people that I have a piece of fur underneath." And this is what he had done, and, although it was a necessity on account of his illnesses, he did not wear it long. (The Assisi Compilation, Section 82)

ST. FRANCIS CONSIDERED a lie to be more than just a spoken or written untruth. He never wanted to give a false impression of holiness to others about anything. He wanted his example to be one of humility, simplicity, love of God, and honesty. Therefore, if he felt that people held him in higher esteem than he deserved, he was quick to point it out to them.

Francis also wanted his brothers to be honest with one another. They were to tell each other what they needed. If they had bad thoughts against others, they were to confess their thoughts to them. He would tolerate no deceit in any fashion among the brothers.

In worldly life, honesty is often a word more than a practice. We are not necessarily referring to cheating on one's income taxes or saying that someone looks beautiful when we think their appearance strange. We are talking about being honest with ourselves first. Who are you really? Have you ever confronted yourself honestly? Are you afraid to do so? Remember that God knows you better than you know yourself, and He has accepted you and loves you with all your faults. So, the first step in being honest with others is to be honest with ourselves.

In our dealings with others, honesty refers to the Commandment, "Thou shalt not bear false witness against thy neighbor." This means not only telling the truth but also taking off the mask about who we are. The mask gives false witness, not about the neighbor but about us. The incident regarding the fox fur is an example of Francis taking off the mask for the public who venerated him as an austere and holy man. He wanted to show them that he was not as austere as they thought. What words or impressions do you leave with others that are not completely based on the truth? How can you rectify this?

When we act with honesty, we must always remember charity. Brutal honesty, in the sense of telling someone exactly what we think, is often uncharitable. If someone asks us if we like something, there is a difference between saying, "I can't stand it!" and saying, "I am sure others like it, but it's not to my taste." Both of these statements are honest. A dishonest statement would be, "Oh, I think it's wonderful!" We can be honest without being cruel.

Spend a minimum of five minutes meditating on the Virtue of Honesty. Do not write anything during this time. Merely begin your time by praying, "Lord, I desire to follow You. Your commandments have asked us to be honest. Grant me the grace to see where I am being honest and where I am being dishonest. Give me the courage and the charity to be honest in all my dealings. Amen."

At the end of your meditation time, ask yourself:

When am I most honest? When do I struggle with honesty? How can I be honest while remaining charitable?

What is my mask? Am I afraid to take it off? Should I? If I should, what graces do I need to do so?

Find another section in Scripture which illustrates the Virtue of Honesty. Find a statement of Jesus or an incident in His life that deals with the Virtue of Honesty. Write these into your journal.

If you are a member of a Religious Order, find one place in your Rule or Constitutions which calls for the Virtue of Honesty. Explain why you chose this section.

Practice the Virtue of Honesty this week. Record in your journal any memorable insights or happenings.

Each evening, examine your day for the times when you were honest and when you could have been more honest. Pray each night, "My Lord, make me an honest person in my thoughts about myself and others and in all my actions, whether they involve me alone or include others. Help me to realize that You know the truth and are waiting for me to display it. Amen."

At the end of the week, record in your journal what you have learned from this exercise.

CHAPTER 18

Hope

Scripture

For I know the plans I have for you, declares the LORD, plans for welfare and not for evil, to give you a future and a hope. (Jeremiah 29:11)

Writings of Saint Francis

Let us, therefore, have charity and humility and give alms because it washes the stains of our sins from our souls. For, although people lose everything they leave behind in this world, they, nevertheless, carry with them the rewards of charity and the alms they have given for which they will receive a reward and a fitting repayment from the Lord. (Second Version of the Letter to the Faithful)

Incident from the Life of Saint Francis

One day he was marveling at the Lord's mercy in the kindness shown to him. He wished that the Lord would show him the course of life for him and his brothers, and he went to a place of prayer, as he so often did. He remained there a long time with fear and trembling before the Ruler of the whole earth. He recalled in the bitterness of his soul the years he spent badly, frequently repeating the phrase: "Lord, be merciful to me, a sinner." Gradually, an indescribable joy and tremendous sweetness began to well up deep in his heart.

He began to lose himself; his feelings were pressed together; and that darkness disappeared which fear of sin had gathered in his heart. Certainty of the forgiveness of all his sins poured in, and the assurance of being revived in grace was given to him. Then he was caught up above himself and totally engulfed in light, and, with his inmost soul opened wide, he clearly saw the future. As that

*sweetness and light withdrew, renewed in spirit, he now seemed to be changed into
another man.*

*He returned and said to the brothers with joy: "Be strong, dear brothers, and
rejoice in the Lord. Do not be sad, because you seem so few, and do not let my simplicity or yours discourage you. The Lord has shown me that God will make us grow
into a great multitude, and will spread us to the ends of the earth." (The Life of Saint
Francis by Thomas of Celano, Chapter XI)*

"Hope" is the thing with feathers—
That perches in the soul—
And sings the tune without the words—
And never stops — at all....

So wrote the poet Emily Dickinson. She was trying to tell us that hope can
fly away, but, if it does not, it is continually present encouraging us to continue.
Hope is an underrated virtue, but it is so necessary to live in hope. Scripture tells
us that our hope is not unfounded, because God is with us at all times and works
all things to our good. Our hope is for eternal life, and our hope will be realized.

St. Francis was a man of hope. Many times in his life, he could have despaired, but he kept moving toward the Lord. He knew that eternal life with God
was his ultimate destination and nothing would keep him from that goal as long
as he persisted in his faith and love of God. Hope is more than a student wishing
for a snow storm to cancel school. Hope is not wishing to become a millionaire
overnight. Virtuous hope is directed toward something attainable. It deals with
holding fast to the promise of eternal salvation and love in the presence of God.
Hope is related to optimism and to trust in God's plan. When we believe that
all things work together for our good, then we have hope that this good will be
realized. God assures us that hope in Him is wise.

Spend a minimum of five minutes meditating on the Virtue of Hope. Do
not write anything during this time. Merely begin your time by praying, "Lord,
help me to understand the Virtue of Hope and where I need it in my life."

At the end of your meditation time, ask yourself:

Am I a hopeful person? What do I hope for? What should I hope for? What things have I hoped for that have been attained? What things have been denied? How does my hope survive when I am disappointed? Can God ever disappoint me? Why does Scripture tell us that our hope must be in God?

Find another section in Scripture which illustrates the Virtue of Hope. Find a statement of Jesus or an incident in His life that deals with the Virtue of Hope. Write these into your journal.

If you are a member of a Religious Order, find one place in your Rule or Constitutions which calls for the Virtue of Hope. Explain why you chose this section.

Practice the Virtue of Hope this week. Record in your journal any memorable insights or happenings.

Each evening, examine your day for the times when you were hopeful and the times when you found yourself despairing. Pray each night, "My God, I hope in You. Increase my hope so that I trust You fully with my life. Amen."

At the end of the week, record in your journal what you have learned from this exercise.

CHAPTER 19

Humility

Scripture

When pride comes, then comes disgrace, but wisdom is with the humble. (Proverbs 11: 2)

Writings of Saint Francis

Thus may the servant of God know if he has the Spirit of God: if when the Lord works some good through him, his body—since it is ever at variance with all that is good—is not therefore puffed up; but if he rather becomes viler in his own sight and if he esteems himself less than other men. (Admonition 12)

Incident from the Life of Saint Francis

He was honored by all and merited high marks from everyone. He alone considered himself vile and was the only one to despise himself fervently. Often honored by others, he suffered great sorrow. Shunning human praise, he had someone, as an antidote, revile him. He would call one of the brothers to him, saying, "I command you under obedience to insult me harshly and speak the truth against their lies." When the brother, though unwilling, called him a bore and a useless hired hand, he would smile and clap loudly, saying: "May the Lord bless you, for you are really telling the truth; that is what the son of Pietro Bernardone needs to hear." Speaking in this fashion, he called to mind the humble origins of his birth. (The Life of Saint Francis of Assisi by Thomas of Celano, Chapter XIX)

HUMILITY IS A virtue which, if you think you have it, you don't. Charles de Gaulle put life into perspective when he said, "The graveyards are full of indispensable men." What are you doing now that is so important? What will happen if you die today? Life goes on without us. The very thought of that should keep us humble.

Humility is the virtue that makes us realize that we are finite human beings and not God. Father Frank Pavone is fond of saying, "Everyone has to learn two things in life. 1. There is a God. 2. It's not me." From the histories about St. Francis, the reader comes to understand that Francis, as a young man, had a "big head." He was far from humble. Following his conversion, he worked at keeping himself humble, and he realized that he never fully achieved his makeover into a humble person. Yet he kept trying. Why? Perhaps he realized the truth of what Saint Augustine wrote: *Humility is the foundation of all the other virtues; hence, in the soul in which this virtue does not exist, there cannot be any other virtue except in mere appearance.* Do you believe this is true?

We must realize that God created us good and that He loves us. This gives us worth beyond telling, no matter what anyone says about us. However, God also made everyone else, and He loves them as well. That gives them worth beyond all telling. So all of us are of equal worth, and all of us are creatures of God. Humility is recognizing our place among all others and our place before God. We are His beloved child, along with all His other beloved children.

For many of us, humility is developed only when we think of others as being better, more loving, or more worthy than ourselves. This comparison may or may not be true, but we can become humble by putting others before ourselves. This is what St. Francis did. Putting others first is a great antidote to those suffering the poison of pride.

Spend a minimum of five minutes meditating on the Virtue of Humility. Do not write anything during this time. Merely begin your time by praying, "Lord, I am your creature. I did not make myself. Neither do I know what is best for me. You are my Creator. Help me to think about what that means for me regarding my thoughts and actions toward You and toward others. Amen."

At the end of your meditation time, ask yourself:

Am I a humble person? What makes me think that I am or am not? Do I want to be humble? Am I afraid to be humble? If so, why?

Find another section in Scripture which illustrates the Virtue of Humility. Find a statement of Jesus or an incident in His life that deals with the Virtue of Humility. Write these into your journal.

If you are a member of a Religious Order, find one place in your Rule or Constitutions which calls for the Virtue of Humility. Explain why you chose this section.

Practice the Virtue of Humility this week. For example, when you receive a compliment, turn the praise to someone else who may have inspired you or directed you. When you blunder, don't get angry! Be grateful for the opportunity to show the world that you aren't perfect. Each night, humbly confess to God your failings of the day. Ask for His forgiveness.

Each evening, examine your day for the times when you did or did not display humility. Pray each night, "Lord, grant me an increase of humility. Please grant me the grace to embrace this virtue. Amen."

At the end of the week, record in your journal what you have learned from this exercise.

CHAPTER 20

Imitation Of Jesus

Scripture

"If anyone would come after me, let him deny himself and take up his cross and follow me." (Jesus' words in Mark 8:34)

Writings of Saint Francis

Let us all, brothers, consider the Good Shepherd who to save His sheep bore the suffering of the Cross. The sheep of the Lord followed Him in tribulation and persecution and shame, in hunger and thirst, in infirmity and temptations and in all other ways; and for these things they have received everlasting life from the Lord. Wherefore it is a great shame for us, the servants of God, that, whereas the Saints have practiced works, we should expect to receive honor and glory for reading and preaching the same. (Admonitions 6)

Incident from the Life of Saint Francis

When they saw and heard these things, two men from Assisi, inspired by divine grace, humbly approached him. One of these was brother Bernard, and the other, brother Peter. They told Francis simply: "We wish to live with you from now on and do what you are doing. Tell us, therefore, what we should do with our possessions." Overjoyed at their coming and their resolve he answered them kindly: "Let us go and seek counsel from the Lord."

So they went to one of the city's churches. Upon entering it, they fell on their knees and humbly prayed: "Lord, God, Father of glory, we beg you in Your mercy, show us what we are to do." After finishing the prayer, they asked the priest of the church who was there: "Sir, would you show us the Gospel of our Lord Jesus Christ?"

And, since before this happened none of them knew how to read very well, when the priest opened up the book, they immediately found the passage "If you wish to be perfect go, sell everything you possess and give it to the poor, and you will have a treasure in heaven." Opening up the book a second time, they discovered: "Whoever wishes to come after me. .. ." When he opened the book for the third time, they came upon: "Take nothing for the journey. . ." When they heard this, they were filled with great joy and exclaimed: "This is what we want, this is what we are seeking." And blessed Francis said: "This will be our rule." Then he told both of them: "Go and may you fulfill the Lord's counsel as you heard it." (The Anonymous of Perugia, Chapter II)

St. Francis's entire way of life was based on imitating Jesus. In fact, he was so successful at this that his biographers cast the incidents in his life as reflections of those in Christ's life. He was called by some an "alter Christi." Francis would have shuddered at this comparison. He never felt that he clearly imitated his Savior, but he always tried. He called this "walking in the footprints of Christ." Think about following someone along the beach or through a wet snow. Have you ever tried to walk in their footprints, so that only one set of prints is left in the snow or on the beach instead of two? This is what Francis meant. He would follow Christ so closely that when anyone saw what he left behind, that person would think, not of Francis, but of Jesus.

Jesus is the perfect example, because He is God made man. And as such, He does everything perfectly. Francis knew that if he imitated Jesus, as much as he could in every aspect of life, then he could not help but be holy. He could not help but win God's favor. He could not help but gain eternal life. Francis was not trained as a theologian. Jesus was his book of theology. Everything he did, he compared to the yardstick of Christ. How did he measure up? He did not want to fall short. And so every decision regarding prayer and action was based on "What would Jesus do?" This popular motto among Christian circles a few years ago was embraced by St. Francis centuries ago. However, it was never a fad to him. It was his entire way of life.

Spend a minimum of five minutes meditating on the Virtue of Imitation of Jesus. Do not write anything during this time. Merely begin your time by praying, "My Jesus, I realize that I need to imitate You. I need to constantly ask You what You would do in this situation and then follow Your holy example. Make me attentive to how You would act and give me the courage to follow. Amen."

At the end of your meditation time, ask yourself:

Where am I trying to imitate Jesus in my life? Where have I chosen not to imitate Him? Am I afraid to ask God to make my life more closely conform to that of Christ's? How do I deal with this fear? Do I really want to imitate Jesus? What is holding me back?

Find another section in Scripture which illustrates the Virtue of Imitation of Jesus. Find a statement of Jesus or an incident in His life that deals with the Virtue of Imitation of Jesus. Write these into your journal.

If you are a member of a Religious Order, find one place in your Rule or Constitutions which calls for the Virtue of Imitation of Jesus. Explain why you chose this section.

Practice the Virtue of Imitation of Jesus this week. Record in your journal any memorable insights or happenings.

Each evening, examine your day for the times when you consciously or unconsciously imitated Jesus. Reflect on the times when you clearly did not imitate Him. Ask God's forgiveness for those times. Pray each night, "Lord, I want to follow in Your footsteps. Open my eyes to see how to do this and give my spirit courage to follow through. Amen."

At the end of the week, record in your journal what you have learned from this exercise.

Chapter 21

Joy

Scripture

Though you have not seen him, you love him. Though you do not now see him, you believe in him and rejoice with joy that is inexpressible and filled with glory, obtaining the outcome of your faith, the salvation of your souls. (1 Peter 1:8-9)

Writings of Saint Francis

Wherever the brothers may be and in whatever place they meet, they should respect spiritually and attentively one another, and honor one another without complaining. Let them be careful not to appear outwardly as sad and gloomy hypocrites but show themselves as joyful, cheerful and consistently gracious in the Lord. (Earlier Rule, Chapter VII)

Incident from the Life of Saint Francis

Once while he was singing praises to the Lord in French in a certain forest, thieves suddenly attacked him. When they savagely demanded who he was, the man of God answered confidently and forcefully: "I am the Herald of the great King! What is it to you?" They beat him and threw him into a ditch filled with deep snow, saying: "Lie there, you stupid Herald of God!" After they left, he rolled about to and fro, shook the snow off himself and jumped out of the ditch. Exhilarated with great joy, he began in a loud voice to make the woods resound with praises to the Creator of all. (The Life of Saint Francis by Thomas of Celano, Chapter VII)

JOY, PRAISE, AND love of God always went together in the life of St. Francis. It was impossible for him to experience one of these virtues without experiencing the other two. When we read the life of St. Francis, the word joy strikes us as a consistent word describing Francis and the friars. They found joy in everything, and if they did not find it easily, they looked for it. Francis wanted the friars to show a joyful face to everyone they met, because they were living examples of God's salvation and grace.

A famous incident from the life of St. Francis is entitled "perfect joy." In this incident, Francis and Brother Leo are traveling along the road and Brother Leo asks Francis what is perfect joy. Francis begins to reveal many worldly situations in which the friars make many converts and are held in high esteem. However, Francis tells Brother Leo that this is not perfect joy. Finally, he explains that perfect joy is coming to the friary of his brothers who should have welcomed him with great love but who instead turn him away as a thief and an imposter. On a bitter, cold, and rainy night. Francis ends the story by saying that if he retains his composure and does not get angry, that is perfect joy. The joy is not in being turned away, but in overcoming one's human tendency to anger at those who treated him so badly. Francis can have perfect joy even when he suffers unjustly at the hands of those who should love him, because he knows that his patience under trial will bring the reward of eternal life. He is joyful, because he knows that if he can be patient in this situation, that he is imitating Christ who suffered unjustly at the hands of those who should have loved Him.

Joy is different from happiness. Happiness is a temporal emotion. We may be happy that we got a new job, or that we are eating an ice cream sundae, or that someone told us they liked our new outfit. Joy transcends all this and focuses on our eternal salvation with God. We are joyful because God has created us, has loved us, has redeemed us, and has promised us eternal life. No one can take this joy from us, as Scripture says. As long as we hold fast to our faith, no matter what is happening around us, we can be joyful. We know that God is in charge and God is the ultimate rewarder of all that we do. Thus, joy goes beyond the circumstances to the ultimate goal where all is joy and love in heaven.

Spend a minimum of five minutes meditating on the Virtue of Joy. Do not write anything during this time. Merely begin your time by praying, "My Lord,

I need to understand the Virtue of Joy. Help me to embrace true joy in my life. Amen."

At the end of your meditation time, ask yourself:

Can I call myself a joyful person? Why or why not? If I am not naturally joyful, how can I develop joy? How can I foster joy in difficult situations? Why is joy a virtue? Why was it such an important virtue to St. Francis?

Find another section in Scripture which illustrates the Virtue of Joy. Find a statement of Jesus or an incident in His life that deals with the Virtue of Joy. Write these into your journal.

If you are a member of a Religious Order, find one place in your Rule or Constitutions which calls for the Virtue of Joy. Explain why you chose this section.

Practice the Virtue of Joy this week. Record in your journal any memorable insights or happenings.

Each evening, examine your day for the times when you felt joy and when you did not feel it but should have. Each night, pray, "My Lord, Father, Son, and Holy Spirit, I look at all You have done for me and the world: Your creation, Your salvation, Your constant presence. Grant me the grace to realize the joy in this reality and to find joy always in my life even when I am unhappy. Amen."

At the end of the week, record in your journal what you have learned from this exercise.

CHAPTER 22

Justice

Scripture

"Thus says the Lord of hosts, Render true judgments, show kindness and mercy to one another." (Zechariah 7:9)

Writings of Saint Francis

Let whoever has received the power of judging others pass judgment with mercy, as they would wish to receive mercy from the Lord. For judgment will be without mercy for those who have not shown mercy. (Second Version of the Letter to the Faithful)

Incident from the Life of Saint Francis

At the religion's beginning, when the brothers were staying at Rivo Torto, there was a brother among them who prayed little, did not work, and did not want to go for alms because he was ashamed; but he would eat heartily. Giving the matter some thought, blessed Francis knew through the Holy Spirit that the man was carnal. He therefore told him: "Go on your way, Brother Fly, because you want to feed on the labor of your brothers, but wish to be idle in the work of God, like Brother Drone that does not want to gather or work, yet eats the work and gain of the good bees."

So he went his way. And because he lived according to the flesh, he did not ask for mercy. (The Assisi Compilation, Section 97)

JUSTICE IS DEFINED as "the process or result of using laws to fairly judge and punish crimes and criminals." This means that rules are applied to everyone equally. If the speed limit says 25 mph, you are served a ticket whether or not you are rich or poor or the mayor of the town. Everyone needs to stay within the 25 mile-per-hour limit.

However, Scripture tells us that God, who is perfect, tempers judgment with mercy. We need only think of Christ's sacrificial death on the cross. Certainly it was not just that He Who is perfect died for us sinners, but it was merciful. And God, in His perfection of justice, accepted the sacrifice of His Perfect Son as payment for our exceedingly great sins.

Here is a modern example of mercy tempering justice. Let's say that someone breaks the 25 mile per hour speed limit because he is driving to the hospital someone who is having a heart attack. If a police officer stops the car and sees the man in need of a doctor, he might decline to issue a ticket and escort the car to the hospital himself. Justice does not show favoritism, but it does show compassion.

St. Francis also tempered justice with mercy. The example of Brother Fly shows that Francis realized that it was unjust to support a friar who did nothing to support himself when he was perfectly able to do so. Supporting this lazy friar meant behaving unmercifully toward the other brothers who were working and begging for their food. So when Brother Fly did not change, the only merciful thing to do was to discharge him from the community. And this is what Francis did.

Justice also relates to rejecting bribes that would influence a decision. Children often attempt this tactic. By flattery or by offering their parents some sort of work, they attempt to mitigate any punishment for wrongs which they knowingly have done. Adults, too, use this tactic. They try to worm their way ahead of others by offering some sort of perk to the person responsible for making decisions.

Are you just in how you treat others? Do you expect justice to be directed toward you in every way, or are you looking for favors?

Spend a minimum of five minutes meditating on the Virtue of Justice. Do not write anything during this time. Merely begin your time by praying, "My just God, I sometimes treat others unjustly while expecting others to treat me with leniency. Help me to evaluate justice and its place in my life. Amen."

At the end of your meditation time, ask yourself:

Would I consider myself a just person? Do I offer favoritism to those I like instead of a just decision? Where and when? Do I expect favoritism in my behalf? Do I temper justice with mercy? Why is justice a virtue?

Find another section in Scripture which illustrates the Virtue of Justice. Find a statement of Jesus or an incident in His life that deals with the Virtue of Justice. Write these into your journal.

If you are a member of a Religious Order, find one place in your Rule or Constitutions which calls for the Virtue of Justice. Explain why you chose this section.

Practice the Virtue of Justice this week. Record in your journal any memorable insights or happenings.

Each evening, examine your day for the times when you did or did not practice justice, or when justice was or was not shown to you. Pray each night, "Lord, help me to be just in all my dealings and to expect justice from others. If justice is not shown to me, grant me the patience to accept it. Amen."

At the end of the week, record in your journal what you have learned from this exercise.

CHAPTER 23

Love Of Enemy

Scripture

"You have heard that it was said, 'You shall love your neighbor and hate your enemy.'
"But I say to you, love your enemies and pray for those who persecute you, so that you
may be sons of your Father who is in heaven; for He causes His sun to rise on the evil
and the good, and sends rain on the righteous and the unrighteous." (Matthew 5:43-5)

Writings of Saint Francis

All my brothers: let us pay attention to what the Lord says; love your enemies and
do good to those who hate you for our Lord Jesus Christ, Whose footprints we must
follow, called His betrayer a friend and willingly offered Himself to His executioners.

Our friends, therefore, are all those who unjustly inflict upon us distress and
anguish, shame and injury, sorrow and punishment, martyrdom and death. We
must love them greatly for we shall possess eternal life because of what they bring us.
(Earlier Rule, Chapter XXII)

Incident from the Life of Saint Francis

Now in the 13th year of his conversion, he journeyed to the region of Syria, while bit-
ter and long battles were being waged daily between Christians and pagans. Taking
a companion with him, he was not afraid to present himself to the sight of the Sultan
of the Saracens.. . .

Before he reached the Sultan, he was captured by soldiers, insulted and beaten,
but was not afraid. He did not flinch at threats of torture nor was he shaken by

death threats. Although he was ill treated by many with a hostile spirit and a harsh attitude, he was received very graciously by the Sultan. The Sultan honored him as much as he could, offering him many gifts, trying to turn his mind to worldly riches. But when he saw that he resolutely scorned all these things like dung, the Sultan was overflowing with admiration and recognized him as a man unlike any other. He was moved by his words and listened to him very willingly. (The Life of Saint Francis by Thomas of Celano, Chapter XX)

AT THE TIME of St. Francis, the Christians and Muslims were engaged in a bitter war for control of the Christian holy places in the Middle East. Despite this, Francis refused to see the Muslims as his enemy. He saw them as brothers and sisters in need of finding the true God. So we went to them to tell them about Christ. Francis did not insult the Muslim God or prophet but instead told the Sultan about Jesus and His teachings. The Sultan respected Francis for his respect of others.

Jesus told us to love our enemies. One way of loving them is to show them respect while we pray for their conversion. We may treat them with respect to their faces because not doing so could bring us more persecution. Do we respect them behind their backs? Our enemies have dignity if only because they, too, are made in God's image and likeness, no matter how badly they may have defaced that image.

Loving our enemies means praying for them so that they can enjoy eternal happiness with God. Does it make you shudder to think that your enemy might be in heaven with you? Do you realize, that if that happens, that person will no longer be an enemy but a brother or sister in Christ? Only perfection is allowed in heaven, so whatever character traits have made this person your enemy will be erased before he or she can enter eternal life. When God asks us to love our enemies, He means that we pray for their salvation. Loving an enemy does not necessarily mean putting oneself in danger of being in the presence of that person. That would not be showing respect for our own life and our emotional well-being. However, loving an enemy does mean praying for that person, even if we don't want to.

Spend a minimum of five minutes meditating on the Virtue of Love of Enemy. Do not write anything during this time. Merely begin your time by praying, "My Jesus, You died for those who persecuted You. You loved Your enemies and You died for their salvation. Grant me the grace to follow You in this virtue of Love of Enemies. Amen."

At the end of your meditation time, ask yourself:

Who are my enemies? Why are they my enemies? If you think you have none, think of who you dislike or think of the enemies of others. Now ask yourself: do I pray for that person or persons? Do I talk badly about them? Do I think badly about them? Is it possible for me to love them? How?

Find another section in Scripture which illustrates the Virtue of Love of Enemy. Find a statement of Jesus or an incident in His life that deals with the Virtue of Love of Enemy. Write these into your journal.

If you are a member of a Religious Order, find one place in your Rule or Constitutions which calls for the Virtue of Love of Enemy. Explain why you chose this section.

Practice the Virtue of Love of Enemy this week. Record in your journal any memorable insights or happenings.

Each evening, examine your day for the times when you practiced Love of Enemy and when you were blocked in this virtue. Pray each night, "Lord, make me more like You. Grant me a love for those who do not love me. Help me to want this virtue. Amen."

At the end of the week, record in your journal what you have learned from this exercise.

CHAPTER 24

Love Of God

Scripture

And thou shalt love the LORD thy God with all thine heart, and with all thy soul, and with all thy might. (Deuteronomy 6:5)

Writings of Saint Francis

With our whole heart, our whole soul, our whole mind, with our whole strength and fortitude, with our whole understanding, with all our powers, with every effort, every affection, every feeling, every desire and wish, let us all love the Lord God Who has given and gives to each one of us our whole body, our whole soul and our whole life, Who has created, redeemed and will save us by His mercy alone, Who did and does everything good for us, miserable and wretched, rotten and foul, ungrateful and evil ones. Therefore, let us desire nothing else, let us want nothing else, let nothing else please us and cause us delight except our Creator, Redeemer and Savior, the only true God, Who is the fullness of good, all good, every good, the true and supreme good, Who alone is good, merciful, gentle, delightful, and sweet, Who alone is holy, just, true, holy, and upright, Who alone is kind, innocent, clean, from Whom, through Whom and in Whom is all pardon, all grace, all glory of all penitents and just ones, of all the blessed rejoicing together in heaven. (Earlier Rule, Chapter XXXIII)

Incident from the Life of Saint Francis

He reached a place near Bevagna, in which a great multitude of birds of all different types gathered, including doves, crows, and others commonly called monacle. When Francis, the most blessed servant of God, saw them, he ran swiftly toward them, leaving his companions on the road. He was a man of great fervor, feeling much sweetness and tenderness even toward lesser, irrational creatures. When he was already very close, seeing that they awaited him, he greeted them in his usual way. He was quite surprised, however, because the birds did not take flight, as they usually do. Filled with great joy, he humbly requested that they listen to the word of God.

Among many other things, he said to them: "My brother birds, you should greatly praise your Creator, and love Him always. "...

He was already simple by grace, not by nature. After the birds had listened so reverently to the word of God, he began to accuse himself of negligence because he had not preached to them before. From that day on, he carefully extorted all birds, all animals, all reptiles, and also all insensible creatures, to praise and love the Creator, because daily, invoking the name of the Savior, he observed their obedience in his own experience. (The Life of Saint Francis of Assisi by Thomas of Celano, Chapter XXI)

OF COURSE, I love God, you might be thinking. Yes, of course, you do! Then read the Scripture verse again and read the writing of St. Francis and the incident from his life again. Notice these words: *"with all thine heart, and with all thy soul, and with all thy might."* And these, *"With our whole heart, our whole soul, our whole mind, with our whole strength and fortitude, with our whole understanding, with all our powers, with every effort, every affection, every feeling, every desire and wish."* And this: *"love Him always."* Measure your love of God against these phrases. Do you measure up?

Spend a minimum of five minutes meditating on the Virtue of Love of God. Do not write anything during this time. Merely begin your time by praying, "Lord, help me to love You more, to put You first in my life, and to praise You forever. Increase my love. Amen."

At the end of your meditation time, ask yourself:

Do I love God, or am I just putting on a show? Am I fooling myself by saying that I love God? How do I know if I love Him? Do I love God more than anything else in my life? What comes between me and God? How do I show my love of God to God, to others, and to myself? Am I afraid to love God too much? If so, why?

Find another section in Scripture which illustrates the Virtue of Love of God. Find a statement of Jesus or an incident in His life that deals with the Virtue of Love of God. Write these into your journal.

If you are a member of a Religious Order, find one place in your Rule or Constitutions which calls for the Virtue of Love of God. Explain why you chose this section.

Practice the Virtue of Love of God this week. Record in your journal any memorable insights or happenings.

Each evening, examine your "Love of God" barometer. Is the barometer going up or down? Is it even registering? Pray each night, "Lord, help me to love You fully and to love You constantly. Amen."

At the end of the week, record in your journal what you have learned from this exercise.

CHAPTER 25

Love Of Neighbor

Scripture

For all the law is fulfilled in one word: Thou shalt love thy neighbor as thyself. (Gal. 5:14) Bear one another's burdens; and so you shall fulfil the law of Christ. (Galatians 6:2)

Writings of Saint Francis

The Lord says in the Gospel, "Love your enemies," etc. He truly loves his enemy who does not grieve because of the wrong done to himself, but who is afflicted for love of God because of the sin on his [brother's] soul and who shows his love by his works. (Admonitions 9)

Incident from the Life of Saint Francis

Another time while he was staying at St. Mary of the Portiuncola, a poor old woman who had two sons in religion came to that place seeking some alms of blessed Francis because that year she did not have enough to live.

Blessed Francis said to Brother Peter of Catanio, who was the general minister at the time: "Have we anything to give our mother?" For he used to say that the mother of any brother was his own and that of all of the brothers in the religion. Brother Peter told him: "We do not have anything in the house that we can give her, especially since she wants such alms as would provide for her corporal needs. In the church we only have one New Testament for reading the lessons at matins." At that time, the brothers did not have breviaries and not many psalters.

> *Blessed Francis responded: "Give our mother the New Testament, so she can sell it for her needs. I firmly believe that the Lord and the Blessed Virgin, His Mother, will be pleased more by giving it to her than if you read in it." And so he gave it to her. (The Assisi Compilation, Section 93)*

TODAY'S WORLD IS one of self-centeredness and greed. We are afraid to let go of our excesses, let alone anything we might need ourselves. We anger easily or dismiss those in need. We are afraid to love and get close to others. Love of neighbor begins with the love of God! If we love God we will not find it difficult to love our neighbor as ourselves and we will be willing and able to bear one another's burdens. We will not be judgmental or quick to anger. We will be patient and kind. We will also be able to give from our worldly belongings, from our time, and from the heavenly treasures we store in our hearts! All who come in contact with us will know we are Christians by our love!

Spend a minimum of five minutes meditating on the virtue of Love of Neighbor. Do not write anything during this time. Merely begin by praying, "Lord, help me to understand the Virtue of Love of Neighbor and where I need it in my life."

At the end of your meditation time ask yourself:

Who is my neighbor? Is my neighbor anyone I come in contact with? What sort of neighbors, then, do I have? Do I love my neighbor as myself? Am I willing to give from my own personal belongings to help another, including my enemies? Am I lacking in charity or being selfish and self-serving, instead of sharing my faith, love, material goods and time with others? Am I willing to give and not expect anything in return? Am I patient, understanding, and loving to my neighbor? Do I push my neighbor away, because I don't want to deal with someone else's problems?

Find another section in Scripture which illustrates the Virtue of Love of Neighbor. Find a statement of Jesus or an incident in His life that deals with the Virtue of Love of Neighbor. Write these into your journal.

If you are a member of a Religious Order, find on place in your Rule or Constitutions which calls for the Virtue of Love of Neighbor. Explain why you chose this section.

Each evening, examine the day for the opportunities to show Love of Neighbor and Pray, "Lord, I know that I do not always show compassion, kindness, and a willingness to love my neighbor as myself. I know that I am selfish and not always willing to give so that my neighbor need not suffer so much. I ask that You grant me the grace to be able to give of my time, my material goods, my love and my faith in order to love my neighbor as myself. By my Love of Neighbor, may I give You the glory You so deserve." Amen

At the end of the week, record in your journal what you have learned from this exercise.

CHAPTER 26

Love Of Self

Scripture

"Do nothing from selfishness or conceit, but in humility count others better than yourselves. Let each of you look not only to his own interests, but also to the interests of others." (Philippians 2:3-4)

Writings of St. Francis

With our whole heart, our whole soul, our whole mind, with our whole strength and fortitude, with our whole understanding, with all our powers, with every effort, every affection, every feeling, every desire and wish, let us all love the Lord God Who has given and gives to each one of us our whole body, our whole soul and our whole life, Who has created, redeemed and will save us by His mercy alone, who did and does everything good for us, miserable and wretched, rotten and foul, ungrateful and evil ones. Therefore, let us desire nothing else, let us want nothing else, let nothing else please us and cause us delight except our Creator, Redeemer and Savior, the only true God Who is the fullness of good. . . . (Earlier Rule, Chapter XXIII)

Incident from the Life of Saint Francis

There was a brother called Riccercio, noble in birth and behavior. He placed such trust in the merits of blessed Francis that he believed that anyone who enjoyed the gift of the saint's affection would be worthy of divine grace; any without it would deserve God's wrath. He therefore anxiously longed to obtain the benefit of his intimacy, but he was very fearful that the saint might discover in him some hidden fault and then he would actually be further away from the saint's good will.

These deep fears tormented that brother every day, and he did not reveal his thoughts to anyone. One day, worried as usual, he approached the cell where Saint Francis was praying. The man of God knew of both his coming and his state of mind and called him kindly to himself. "My son," he said, "let no fear or temptation disturb you anymore, for you are very dear to me, and among all those who are dearest to me I love you with a special love. Come to me confidently whenever you want, and leave me freely whenever you want." The brother was extremely shocked and overjoyed at the words of the holy father. From that time on, knowing he was loved, he grew-- as he believed-- in the grace of the Savior. (The Remembrance of the Desire of a Soul by Thomas of Celano, Chapter XV)

IN ORDER TO understand the virtue of Love of Self, we must first understand that without God we are nothing! We cannot serve our neighbor, love others, or do anything good without loving God. We must never boast about the good God does through us as though we are responsible for it on our own.

God sent His only son to die on the cross and to rise again so that we might have eternal life. This alone teaches that Love of Self is never selfish. God loved us enough to die for us, so how can we not love ourselves? God made us and God only creates good, so how can we be anything but loveable? A classic poster reads, "God does not make junk." And God made YOU. God leaves no room for disparaging yourself, only for repentance for any sins committed or blunders made. Making a mistake does not make YOU a mistake. God does not make mistakes, and God made YOU.

If we love ourselves, then we will automatically have humility, patience, kindness, and love for others, because God made them, too. In giving His life for us, Jesus taught us to always put others first, to never count the cost, and to love with no expectations. If you love God with all of your heart, mind and soul, put others before yourself, and deny yourself some of life's pleasures in order to help others, then you will have achieved the virtue of Love of Self in its true meaning!

Spend a minimum of five minutes meditating on the Virtue of Love of Self. Do not write anything during this time. Merely begin your time by praying, "Lord, help me to understand the virtue of Self Love and where I need it in my life."

At the end of your meditation time, ask yourself:

Do I love myself? If I don't, how can I learn to love myself? Why should I love myself? What is the difference between loving myself and being prideful of me? Do I try to practice humility when it comes to criticism, dealing with those less fortunate than myself, or when faced with complaints and anger? Do I love myself enough to try to always put others before myself? Do I love myself so much that I can deny myself some of life's pleasures in order to help others? Do I truly understand that I am nothing without God, and that I can do nothing good without God? Do I brag about the good God does through me as though it were myself doing it? What can I change in my life to help me to have true Love of Self that comes from loving God?

Find another section in Scripture which illustrates the Virtue of Love of Self. Find a statement of Jesus or an incident in His life that deals with the Virtue of Love of Self. Write these in your journal.

If you are a member of a Religious Order, find one place in your Rule or Constitutions which calls for the Virtue of Love of Self. Explain why you chose this section.

Practice the Virtue of Love of Self this week. Find a way to practice humility or to put others above yourself. Deny yourself a simple pleasure and offer it for someone else's suffering. Look at yourself in a mirror and say, "God does not make junk, and God made ME." Record your practice of the Virtue of Love of Self in your journal.

Each evening, examine the day for the opportunities you had to show true Love of Self. Pray, "Lord, please help me to understand the true meaning of Love of Self. I know that I am filled with pride and remiss in denying myself simple pleasures for the sake of others. I also know that sometimes I loathe myself, and I know this is wrong as You don't loathe me. Help me to lower myself enough to accept Your unconditional love. Grant me the grace to love myself deeply enough to always put others before myself and to deny myself so that others may have what they need. Help me to become small so that You may increase! I ask this in the name of Jesus Christ, Your Son. Amen"

At the end of the week, record in your journal what you have learned from this exercise.

CHAPTER 27

Loyalty To Church

Scripture

"Brothers, I beg you to be on the watch against those who cause dissension and scandal, contrary to the teaching you have received. Avoid their company. Such men serve, not Christ our Lord, but their own bellies and they deceive the simpleminded with smooth and flattering speech." (Romans 16:17-18)

Writings of Saint Francis

All the brothers must be Catholics, [and] live and speak in a Catholic manner. But if any of them has strayed from the Catholic faith, in word or in deed, and has not amended his ways, he should be completely expelled from our fraternity. And we should regard all clerics and all religious as our Lord in those things which pertain to the salvation of the soul and who have not deviated from our religion, and, in the Lord, we should respect their order and their office and government. (Saint Francis of Assisi, Earlier Rule, Chapter XIX)

Incident from the Life of Saint Francis

He used to revere prelates and priests of the holy Church. . . . He zealously used to admonish [his brothers] to observe the holy Gospel and the Rule conscientiously as they had promised: and especially to be reverent toward ecclesiastical offices and regulations: to be attentive and devoted when hearing Mass, and when they saw the Body of our Lord Jesus Christ. They were to have reverence toward priests who handle these tremendous and greatest sacraments and, whenever they encountered them, they were to bow their heads to them and kiss their hands. If they found them on horseback, they were to make a sign of reverence, kissing not only the hands of a priest, but, out of reverence for their power, even the hooves of their horses. (The Anonymous of Perugia, Chapter VIII)

ONE OF ST. Francis's biographers called him "a thoroughly Catholic man." At the time of Francis's conversion, the Catholic Church was not highly respected by the populace. Many priests were not well trained and gave no sermons to instruct the people. Some of the clergy were involved in simony and sexual infractions. Others lived lives of luxury at the expense of the poor. Heretics abounded who lived austere, poor lives and who were preaching the faith with their own twist on it. People were searching for a church whose members practiced what they preached. Despite the religious confusion and his society, St. Francis remained loyal to the Church, because he believed that Jesus had founded it and was guiding it.

Francis's loyalty to the church kept his ragtag Friars from being dismissed as disloyal heretics. Francis assured the Pope of his loyalty and the Pope could see that he was sincere. Never did Francis condemn the church or any of its priests or other clergy. He always said that the priests were the ones who consecrated the Body of Christ and deserved our respect for that reason, no matter what behaviors they may have been involved in. Loyalty to the Church under this duress required heroic virtue from the Holy Spirit.

We note that even Peter and the apostles struggled with loyalty. After having confidently professed their loyalty in the quiet room of the Last Supper, they quickly fled from supporting Jesus when faced with the reality of armed soldiers in the garden of Gethsemane. Fear and cowardice replaced the devotion in the upper room.

We know how the passion played out. Peter wept and went on to assume his role as head of the apostles and a martyr of the faith. Judas despaired of his disloyalty and hung himself. John the evangelist reclaimed his loyalty quickly and was at the foot of the cross with the Blessed mother whose loyalty never failed. We can learn much about loyalty from each of these key members in the life of Christ.

From the examples of the apostles, we can learn that, if we have been disloyal to the Church by ignoring or even speaking against some of its doctrines or authorities, we have one of two choices to make. Either we can repent of our disloyalty as Peter did and return to the Church, or we can distance ourselves from the Church as did Judas and never return to it again. Or, as soon as we sense any sort of disloyalty creeping in, we can immediately turn to spiritual guidance to answer our questions of "why" and "what" and reclaim our loyalty as did John, even as we wait for our questions to be answered. God be praised if our loyalty has been, is, and will continue to be as solid as that of Our Lady, whose loyalty never failed!

Spend a minimum of five minutes meditating on the Virtue of Loyalty to the Church. Do not write anything during this time. Merely begin your time by praying, "Lord, help me to understand the virtue of Loyalty to the Church and where I need it or have it in my life."

At the end of your meditation time, ask yourself:

Am I making compromises in my practice of the faith? Do I neglect to defend truth because of fear of human opinion or convenience? Do I remain silent during attacks on the faith? Why? Do I need more knowledge to defend the faith? Do I defend the faith aggressively but fail to listen to the actual difficulties and misunderstandings people have about the Catholic Church? Am I reverent at Mass? Am I attentive, on time, and silent? How reverent am I in regard to the sacraments, my prayer life, the name and person of Jesus, the Blessed Mother, or my Rule (member of Religious Order)? Have I become lukewarm? Do I experience dryness? Do temptations weaken my devotion? How far would I go to defend my faith? Am I willing to give up material gain, social status, or my life as a witness of my love for Jesus and His Church? How strong is my relationship with the Blessed Mother? How do loyalty to the Catholic Church and devotion to the Blessed Mother worked together?

Find another section in Scripture which illustrates the Virtue of Loyalty to the Church. Find a statement of Jesus or an incident in His life that deals with the Virtue of Loyalty to the Church (since Jesus established the Church, the passage may relate more to loyalty to God). Write these in your journal.

If you are a member of a Religious Order, find one place in your Rule or Constitutions which calls for the Virtue of Loyalty to the Church. Explain why you chose this section.

Practice the Virtue of Loyalty to the Church this week. For example, pray for the Church daily. Ask God's Spirit to guide all those in authority in the Church. Refer to the Catechism of the Catholic Church to answer your questions about its teachings. If you see, hear, or read of an attack on the Church and its doctrines, defend the faith in speech or the written word. Also, be charitable and pray for the attackers. Record your practice of the Virtue of Loyalty to the Church in your journal.

Each evening, examine the day for the opportunities you had to show Loyalty to the Church. Pray "Lord, I believe in You. I want to be loyal to the Church that You founded. Give me courage to defend the faith and give me the right words to do so. Give me knowledge where I am deficient and courage where I am fearful. I trust in Your grace, my God. Amen."

At the end of the week, record in your journal what you have learned from this exercise.

CHAPTER 28

Marian Devotion

Scripture

So when the dragon saw that he had been thrown down to the earth, he pursued the woman who had given birth to the male child. But the woman was given the two wings of the great eagle, so that she could fly from the serpent into the wilderness, to her place where she is nourished for a time, and times, and half a time. Then from his mouth the serpent poured water like a river after the woman, to sweep her away with the flood. But the earth came to the help of the woman; it opened its mouth and swallowed the river that the dragon had poured from his mouth. Then the dragon was angry with the woman, and went off to make war on the rest of her children, those who keep the commandments of God and hold the testimony of Jesus. (Revelations 12:13-17)

Writings of Saint Francis

Hail, O Lady, Holy Queen,
Mary, holy Mother of God,
Who are the Virgin made Church,
chosen by the most Holy Father in heaven
whom he consecrated with His most holy beloved Son
and with the Holy Spirit the Paraclete,
in whom there was and is
all fullness of grace and every good.
Hail His Palace!
Hail His Tabernacle!
Hail His Dwelling!
Hail His Robe!

Hail His Servant!
Hail His Mother!
And hail all You holy virtues
which are poured into the hearts of the faithful
through the grace and enlightenment of the Holy Spirit,
that from being unbelievers,
You may make them faithful to God. (Salutation of the Blessed Virgin Mary)

Incident from the Life of Saint Francis

He embraced the Mother of Jesus with inexpressible love, since she made the Lord of Majesty a brother to us. He honored her with his own Praises, poured out prayers to her, and offered her his love in a way that no human tongue can express. But what gives us greatest joy is that he appointed her the Advocate of the Order, and placed under her wings the sons to be left behind, that she might protect and cherish them to the end. (The Remembrance of the Desire of a Soul by Thomas of Celano, Chapter CL)

SAINT FRANCIS HAD a tremendous devotion to the Blessed Mother, perhaps as a result of his devotion to his earthly mother who steadfastly showed him love and support. Francis knew the comfort of a mother's love and attention.

The Scripture selection describes the war of the serpent (Satan) on the woman (Blessed Mother) and her children (we poor humans). If we honor Christ, certainly we would want to also honor His Mother. After all, she birthed, nurtured, and taught Him as a child. She was with Him through His public ministry and through His Passion. From the cross, Jesus gave His Mother to the world when He gave her into the care of the apostle John.

The world, the flesh, and the devil tend to minimize the devotion which we should owe to the Blessed Mother. Devotion to Mary, like devotion to our earthy mothers, does not mean worship of her. Devotion means loving her and asking her intercession, for who would be a more powerful intercessor with any good man than his good mother? Like Saint Francis, those who cultivate a devotion to Mary come to recognize the beauty, the generosity, the mercy, and the wealth of assistance she can give. Since the Blessed Mother was immaculately conceived and is the apex of all virtue, she is the best human teacher and intercessor in our spiritual journey.

Marian Devotion is a virtue that, if practiced, will lead to the development and support of all the other virtues which Our Lady possessed in high degree. Take a quick look at the virtues covered in this book. Are there any that Our Lady did not possess?

Spend a minimum of five minutes meditating on the Virtue of Marian Devotion. Do not write anything during this time. Merely begin your time by praying, "Lord, help me to understand the Virtue of Marian Devotion. Please show me if I have this devotion or if I need it more in my life."

At the end of your meditation time, ask yourself:

Do I think of, ask for, or reflect on the assistance of Mary in daily life? Have there been situations where I have succumbed to abruptness, impatience, lack of attentiveness or devotion and could have asked Mary to show me a better way? Has my relationship with Mary become routine or cooled because of distracted-ness or concerns? Am I consecrated to the Blessed Mother? If so, do I renew my consecration yearly through thirty days of preparation? Why is devotion to the Blessed Mother key to being a Catholic? Is it possible to have excessive devotion to the Blessed Mother? Why or why not? Do I take time to thank Mary for all the graces received through her protection and intercession?

Find another section in Scripture which illustrates the Virtue of Marion Devotion. Find a statement of Jesus or an incident in His life that deals with the Virtue of Marion Devotion. Write these into your journal.

If you are a member of a Religious Order, find one place in your Rule or Constitutions which calls for the Virtue of Marion Devotion. Explain why you chose this section.

Practice the Virtue of Marion Devotion this week. Record in your journal any memorable insights or happenings.

Each evening, examine the day for the times you practiced devotion to the Blessed Mother. If you had none of these times, ask yourself why not. Pray," Lord, help me to develop a properly ordered devotion to Your Mother. Give me the love for her that You had. Help me to trust in her powerful intercession for my needs and the needs of the world. Give me the grace to be a devoted child of hers. Amen."

At the end of the week, record in your journal what you have learned from this exercise.

CHAPTER 29

Minority

Scripture

"But, when you are invited, go and recline at the last place, so that when the one who has invited you comes, he may say to you, 'Friend, move up higher'; then you will have honor in the sight of all who are at the table with you." (Luke 14:10)

Writings of St. Francis

They must rejoice when they live among people considered of little value and looked down upon, among the poor and the powerless, the sick and the lepers, and the beggars by the wayside. (Earlier Rule, Chapter IX)

Incident from the Life of Saint Francis

The followers of most holy Poverty, having nothing, loved nothing, and therefore had no fear of losing anything. They were content with a tunic only, patched sometimes within and without; no elegance was seen in it, but great abjectness and vileness, to the end they might wholly appear therein as crucified to the world. They were girt with a cord, and wore drawers of common stuff, and they were piously intent upon remaining in that state, and to have nothing more. Everywhere, therefore, they were secure, nor kept in suspense by any fear, distracted by no care, they awaited the morrow without solicitude, nor, though oftentimes in great straits in their journeys, were they ever in anxiety about a night's lodging. For when, as often happened, they lacked a lodging in the coldest weather, an oven sheltered them, or, at least, they lay hid by night humbly in underground places or in caves. And by day those who knew how to, worked with their hands, and they stayed in lepers' houses, or in other decent places, serving all with humility and devotion. (The Life of Saint Francis by Thomas of Celano, Chapter XV)

HAVE YOU EVER known someone who had just bought a shiny new car, but their anxiety, that someone or something would come along and damage it, completely stole their joy? Ironically, was the car actually damaged later on?

Then again, have you ever heard of someone who was famous or wealthy who lost everything or fell from grace, and the humiliation involved?

Have you ever pondered on the size of the burdens carried by people such as heads of state, CEO's of companies, surgeons and others with influential positions? Have you ever said to yourself, "I am glad I don't have that responsibility?"

The less we have, the less there is to lose.

Minority is a virtue that helps us take the lower place willingly. It helps us hold everything loosely so that no thing or attitude or pride possesses us. If we think of ourselves as lesser, we can take insults and disappointments in stride, because we realize that we and our desires and possessions are not more important than anyone else's.

Spend a minimum of five minutes meditating on the Virtue of Minority. Do not write anything during this time. Merely begin your time by praying, "Lord, help me to understand the Virtue of Minority and where I need it in my life."

At the end of your meditation time, ask yourself:

What do I possess that would cause shame or humility to me if I lost it (this goes for reputation and position as well as possessions)? Do I compliment or defend others, or criticize their faults and participate in others' negative comments when the person in question is not present? When criticized, do I become angry and defensive, or do I praise God for the insight and opportunity to change for the better? If it is undeserved criticism or ridicule, do I become indignant, rushing to my own defense or becoming vengeful, or do I take it quietly and offer it up as penance?

Find another section in Scripture which illustrates the Virtue of Minority. Find a statement of Jesus or an incident in His life that deals with the Virtue of Minority. Write these into your journal.

If you are a member of a Religious Order, find one place in your Rule or Constitutions which calls for the Virtue of Minority. Explain why you chose this section.

Practice the Virtue of Minority this week. Record in your journal any memorable insights or happenings.

Each evening consider how well you practiced Minority that day. Are you having trouble seeing yourself in the lowest place? Pray each night, "Lord, help me to assume an attitude of Minority. Make me aware of those times when I am embracing pride instead of lowliness and help me to do better. Amen."

At the end of the week, record in your journal what you have learned from this exercise.

CHAPTER 30

Obedience

Scipture

But he said, "Blessed rather are those who hear the word of God and obey it!" (Luke 11:28)

Writings of Saint Francis

The Lord says in the Gospel: he "that doth not renounce all that he possesseth cannot be" a "disciple " and "he that will save his life, shall lose it." That man leaves all he possesses and loses his body and his soul who abandons himself wholly to obedience in the hands of his superior, and whatever he does and says—provided he himself knows that what he does is good and not contrary to his [the superior's] will—is true obedience. And if at times a subject sees things which would be better or more useful to his soul than those which the superior commands him, let him sacrifice his will to God, let him strive to fulfil the work enjoined by the superior. This is true and charitable obedience which is pleasing to God and to one's neighbor.

If, however, a superior command anything to a subject that is against his soul it is permissible for him to disobey, but he must not leave him [the superior], and if in consequence he suffer persecution from some, he should love them the more for God's sake. For he who would rather suffer persecution than wish to be separated from his brethren, truly abides in perfect obedience because he lays down his life for his brothers. For there are many religious who, under pretext of seeing better things than those which their superiors command, look back and return to the vomit of their own will. These are homicides and by their bad example cause the loss of many souls. (Admonition 3)

Incident from the Life of Saint Francis

Although he was more exalted than all other brothers, he still appointed one of the brothers staying with him as his guardian and master. He humbly and devoutly obeyed him, in order to avoid any location of pride. Among people this saint lowered his head even to the ground, and for this the Lord lifted him on high among the saints and elect in heaven. (The Anonymous of Perugia, Chapter VIII)

THE WORD, OBEY, comes from the Latin word *oboedire* which means to hear or heed. In the modern sense, it is to comply with a demand. As children we are taught early to obey our parents, teachers, and police, etc., because they have our best interest in mind. As we grow, our own wills take over. In addition, we come to realize authority figures are not always as concerned with our well-being as we were led to believe. As adults, it takes a great deal of confidence in the providence of God to obey both that still, small voice within us as well as God's representatives on earth. Yet, our salvation depends on it.

We find it easier to obey when our earthly welfare depends on it; in fact, at those times we don't even think about obedience. rarely think about obedience, when our welfare depends on it. The boss tells us to be at work at a certain time, and, no matter how much trouble it is to meet the time frame, we get to work on time, because, if we don't, we'll be jobless. However, when we could get away with not obeying, are we still conscientious? If we can drive over the speed limit a bit and not get caught, if we can manipulate our taxes, if we can cheat on a diet, do we do these things?

Spend a minimum of five minutes meditating on the Virtue of Obedience. Do not write anything during this time. Merely begin by praying, "Lord, help me to understand the Virtue of Obedience and where I need to change my life."

At the end of your meditation time, ask yourself:

Have there been times when I have disobeyed God to avoid loss of human respect or the good graces of another person? When these incidents happened, what prompted me to choose that path? Was it a lack of awareness of the right thing to do or simply a fear of the unpleasant consequences? Was I just seeking the approval of my peers? Did I think I knew better than God what was good for me?

Is there an area of my life where I am continuing to disobey God? What do I need to change in order to be compliant with His precepts? Do I have the will to make those changes? It takes detachment from the need for human respect to find the courage to make those changes. What would I need to detach myself from to comply with the Will of God?

How do I find out what God's instructions are? The Church teaches, through the catechism, that God's Will is found through Holy Scripture and the legitimate representatives of His Church. It can also be found through our family and social relationships when they have rightful authority over us. Do I accept this? Are there areas that I struggle with compliance?

Find another section in Scripture which illustrates the Virtue of Obedience. Find a statement of Jesus or an incident in His life that deals with the Virtue of Obedience. Write these into your journal.

If you are a member of a Religious Order, find one place in your Rule or Constitutions which calls for the Virtue of Obedience. Explain why you chose this section.

Practice the Virtue of Obedience this week. Pride and disobedience go together, according to St. Francis and the Fathers of the Church; therefore, obedience requires the cultivation of the Virtue of Humility. The saints have these two virtues in common, and to a high degree. What act of humility can I perform that will help me to grow in obedience?

To counter a sin or vice, say many great saints of the Church, a good remedy is to practice the opposite virtue in an exaggerated way. What one activity can I do to demonstrate my obedience to God's Will? For example, if I have willfully missed Mass, can I begin to go to daily Mass, or can I participate more fully as a lector, choir member, or sacristan?

As you practice the Virtue of Obedience daily, record in your journal any memorable insights or happenings.

Each evening ask yourself, "How was I obedient today? Where was I disobedient? How could I have done better? What was my attitude toward obeying?" Pray each night, "Lord, help me to become more willingly and joyfully obedient. Amen."

At the end of the week, record in your journal what you have learned from this exercise.

CHAPTER 31

Pardon

Scripture

Then Peter came and said to Him, "Lord, how often shall my brother sin against me and I forgive him? Up to seven times?" Jesus said to him, "I do not say to you, up to seven times, but up to seventy times seven. (Matthew 18:21-22)

Writings of Saint Francis

Praised be You, my Lord, through those who give pardon for Your love,
and bear infirmity and tribulation.
Blessed are those who endure in peace
for by You, Most High, shall they be crowned. (Canticle of the Creatures)

Incident from the Life of Saint Francis

He was then rejected by his own fellow citizens who threw mud at him; he was struck by stones, but fixing his mind on God alone, he made himself dead to all these events. (The Legend for Use in the Choir by Thomas of Celano, Section I)

DO YOU HAVE someone with whom you are angry? Maybe someone at work? Or that driver on the road this morning? Or the abortionist? Or the public official who fails to speak out against the evil of killing babies? Or might it be someone who deeply hurt you or someone else through betrayal, lies, or abuse?

Whether your hatred is directed toward a driver, a friend, a family member, or a public official, anger and hatred are corrosive – not so much to the person against whom the hate is directed but to the person harboring the hatred. Pardoning those people – and praying for them – will change your life. You may still be disappointed that a public official doesn't speak out again abortion, but the hatred that eats at you will disappear. You may still carry the wounds of the harm inflicted on you by another, but pardoning that person will not justify the abuse. Rather, pardon will redeem the abuse by calling your prayers down upon the one who harmed you and asking God to grace that person with repentance.

The saying goes, "To err is human; to forgive, divine." God calls to forgive others their offenses as He forgives us ours. Don't we pray that very thing in the Lord's Prayer? "And forgive us our trespasses as we forgive those who trespass against us." Are we asking God not to forgive us if we don't forgive others? Think about it!

Spend a minimum of five minutes meditating on the Virtue of Pardon. Do not write anything during this time. Merely begin your time by praying, "Lord, help me to understand the Virtue of Pardon and where I need it in my life."

At the end of your meditation time, ask yourself: What needs my pardon? Who needs my pardon? Am I attentive that situation and to that person? Have I pardoned that person? How can I do better in pardoning others?

Find another section in Scripture which illustrates the Virtue of Pardon. Find a statement of Jesus or an incident in His life that deals with the Virtue of Pardon. Write these into your journal.

If you are a member of a Religious Order, find one place in your Rule or Constitutions which calls for the Virtue of Pardon. Explain why you chose this section.

Practice the Virtue of Pardon this week. First, think of anyone who needs your forgiveness. Can you contact that person or those persons and say you are sorry? If it's impossible or imprudent to do so, mentally tell them that you forgive them. Record in your journal any memorable insights or happenings.

Each evening, examine your day for the times that needed your pardon and for the times when you forgave or did not forgive offenses. Pray each night, "Lord, establish the Virtue of Pardon in my soul so that every offense receives my forgiveness at the moment it occurs. Should I find myself harboring bitterness at any time, give the grace right then to forgive and to pray for Your grace to fall upon the offender. Amen."

At the end of the week, record in your journal what you have learned from this exercise.

CHAPTER 32

Patience

Scripture

For the revelation awaits an appointed time; it speaks of the end and will not prove false. Though it linger, wait for it; it will certainly come and will not delay. (Habakkuk 2:3)

Writings of Saint Francis

How much interior patience and humility a servant of God may have cannot be known so long as he is contented. But when the time comes that those who ought to please him go against him, as much patience and humility as he then shows, so much has he and no more. (Admonitions 13)

Incident from the Life of Saint Francis

How Saint Francis, walking one day with brother Leo, explained to him what things are perfect joy.

One day in winter, as Saint Francis was going with Brother Leo from Perugia to Saint Mary of the Angels, and was suffering greatly from the cold, he called to Brother Leo, who was walking on before him, and said to him: "Brother Leo, if it were to please God that the Friars Minor should give, in all lands, a great example of holiness and edification, write down, and note carefully, that this would not be perfect joy."

A little further on, Saint Francis called to him a second time: "O Brother Leo, if the Friars Minor were to make the lame to walk, if they should make straight the crooked, chase away demons, give sight to the blind, hearing to the deaf, speech to the *dumb, and, what is even a far greater work, if they should raise the dead after four days, write that this would not be perfect joy."*

Shortly after, he cried out again: "O Brother Leo, if the Friars Minor knew all languages; if they were versed in all science; if they could explain all Scripture; if they had the gift of prophecy, and could reveal, not only all future things, but likewise the secrets of all consciences and all souls, write that this would not be perfect joy."

After proceeding a few steps farther, he cried out again with a loud voice: "O Brother Leo, thou little lamb of God! if the Friars Minor could speak with the tongues of angels; if they could explain the course of the stars; if they knew the virtues of all plants; if all the treasures of the earth were revealed to them; if they were acquainted with the various qualities of all birds, of all fish, of all animals, of men, of trees, of stones, of roots, and of waters - write that this would not be perfect joy."

Shortly after, he cried out again: "O Brother Leo, if the Friars Minor had the gift of preaching so as to convert all infidels to the faith of Christ, write that this would not be perfect joy."

Now when this manner of discourse had lasted for the space of two miles, Brother Leo wondered much within himself; and, questioning the saint, he said: "Father, I pray thee teach me wherein is perfect joy." Saint Francis answered: "If, when we shall arrive at Saint Mary of the Angels, all drenched with rain and trembling with cold, all covered with mud and exhausted from hunger; if, when we knock at the convent-gate, the porter should come angrily and ask us who we are; if, after we have told him, "We are two of the brethren", he should answer angrily, "What ye say is not the truth; ye are but two impostors going about to deceive the world, and take away the alms of the poor; begone I say"; if then he refuse to open to us, and leave us outside, exposed to the snow and rain, suffering from cold and hunger till nightfall - then, if we accept such injustice, such cruelty and such contempt with patience, without being ruffled and without murmuring, believing with humility and charity that the porter really knows us, and that it is God who maketh him to speak thus against us, write down, O Brother Leo, that this is perfect joy.

And if we knock again, and the porter come out in anger to drive us away with oaths and blows, as if we were vile impostors, saying, "Begone, miserable robbers! to to the hospital, for here you shall neither eat nor sleep!" - and if we accept all this with patience, with joy, and with charity, O Brother Leo, write that this indeed is perfect joy.

And if, urged by cold and hunger, we knock again, calling to the porter and entreating him with many tears to open to us and give us shelter, for the love of God, and if he come out more angry than before, exclaiming, "These are but importunate rascals, I will deal with them as they deserve"; and taking a knotted stick, he seize us by the hood, throwing us on the ground, rolling us in the snow, and shall beat and wound us with the knots in the stick - if we bear all these injuries with patience and joy, thinking of the sufferings of our Blessed Lord, which we would share out of love for Him, write, O Brother Leo, that here, finally, is perfect joy.

And now, brother, listen to the conclusion. Above all the graces and all the gifts of the Holy Spirit which Christ grants to his friends, is the grace of overcoming oneself, and accepting willingly, out of love for Christ, all suffering, injury, discomfort and contempt; for in all other gifts of God we cannot glory, seeing they proceed not from ourselves but from God, according to the words of the Apostle, "What hast thou that thou hast not received from God? and if thou hast received it, why dost thou glory as if thou hadst not received it?" But in the cross of tribulation and affliction we may glory, because, as the Apostle says again, "I will not glory save in the cross of our Lord Jesus Christ." Amen."

To the praise and glory of Jesus Christ and his poor servant Francis. Amen. (Undated text of Saint Francis from 14th century)

PATIENCE MEANS WAITING, and most of us don't like to wait! The old maximum, "Patience is a virtue" seems to wear a bit thin when we are in the doctor's office two hours and still have not been called into the examining room. We can be ready to give up on patience when our teens leave the shower in shambles, despite being told for the umpteenth time that they are to wipe it down and hang up their towels before leaving.

How many opportunities we have to exercise the Virtue of Patience! At this writing (2016) it has been 43 years since the U.S. Supreme Court declared a woman has a right to kill the baby in her womb. It has been 42 years since the first March for Life, and still abortion is enshrined as a legal procedure in the United States. People have been waiting and working all this time to return protection to the unborn. Pro-lifers take courage from the abolitionists who fought eighty-seven years to do away with slavery in the United States. It takes patience to fight wrongs that never should have happened in the first place.

It's not just dramatic public policy episodes that give us an opportunity to exercise the Virtue of Patience. Has anyone made a snarky remark because you wear a visible cross? That's an opportunity to exercise the virtue of patience, and to pray for that person's conversion. Are you stuck behind a slow-moving car in traffic when you're in hurry? That's an opportunity to exercise the Virtue of Patience. Has anyone made a remark to you that cut you to the quick? That's an opportunity to practice the Virtue of Patience.

Spend a minimum of five minutes meditating on the Virtue of Patience. Do not write anything during this time.

Merely begin your time by praying, "Lord, help me to understand the Virtue of Patience and where I need it in my life."

At the end of your meditation time, ask yourself: Do I exercise the virtue of patience in my life? If not, how can I begin? If I am patient, or think I am, how can I do better? Do I really want to be patient? Do I understand that, if I pray to be patient, God will multiply the opportunities for me to practice this virtue?

Find another section in Scripture which illustrates the Virtue of Patience. Find a statement of Jesus or an incident in His life that deals with the Virtue of Patience. Write these into your journal.

If you are a member of a Religious Order, find one place in your Rule or Constitutions which calls for the Virtue of Patience. Explain why you chose this section.

Practice the Virtue of Patience this week. When something upsets you, try counting to ten before responding. In those ten seconds, you will remember that you are working on being more patient. Ask the Lord to answer your prayer for patience and then respond. Pray, "Lord, give me patience as I practice the Virtue of Patience. I know that You desire this virtue in my life. Multiply the times that I may practice it. Amen."

At the end of the week, record in your journal what you have learned from this exercise.

CHAPTER 33

Peace

Scripture
"Peace I leave with you; my peace I give you. I do not give to you as the world gives. Do not let your hearts be troubled and do not be afraid." (John 14: 27)

Writings of Saint Francis
The Lord revealed a greeting to me that we should say: "May the Lord give you peace." (The Testament)

Incident from the Life of Saint Francis
In all of his preaching, before he presented the word of God to the assembly, he prayed for peace saying, "May the Lord give you peace." He always proclaimed this to men and women, to those he met and to those who met him. Accordingly, many who hated peace along with salvation, with the Lord's help wholeheartedly embraced peace. They became themselves children of peace, now rivals for eternal salvation. (The Life of Saint Francis by Thomas of Celano, Chapter X)

IN THE FACE of wars and insurrections worldwide, we often feel as if peace making is simply beyond our control. It's the task of world leaders to make and keep peace, not ourselves, but that is not the case at all.

It takes people to make war. And it takes people to make peace. If we begin to think of our daily lives and the people in them, we will find among these folks some who are not at peace with others. Maybe one of those people is you!

Peace does not just happen. It must be worked at and worked through. It takes two to make peace. One to extend the olive branch and the other to take it. Saint Francis encouraged all people to extend the olive branch just as he encouraged all people to take it.

How can you offer peace to someone else? How about beginning with an apology and offering an understanding and listening ear? You may get an earful, but embrace the virtue of humility and let the vitriol pass over you. Then say, "Thanks for sharing that. I'm sorry you feel that way. I would like to move on from here and be friends."

How can you accept an offer of peace from someone else when you feel that you have been wronged and maligned? You just accept it. You put behind yourself the self-righteousness an accusation and move forward.

Jesus offered "Blessed are the peacemakers" as one of the Beatitudes. Peacemakers not only arrange peace between warring parties; they may also be one of those parties who want to end the war. Can you see yourself as a peacemaker? Are you in a relationship that needs a peaceful solution? Or do you have a relationship that you are in that needs a peaceful solution? Have you refused to make peace with someone? Has someone refused to make peace with you? Can you return to this person now and attempt to make peace? Can you pray for the offending party? Would Jesus want you to do at least that?

Are you at peace with yourself? If you are troubled, can you speak to a confidant, spiritual friend, priest, or director about your inner turmoil? When we are not at peace with ourselves, it is generally because we do not trust God with our lives. We do not trust Him to forgive, to forget, to heal, to sustain, or to guide. Where is your lack of inner peace coming from? Where do you need to trust God more?

Spend a minimum of five minutes meditating on the Virtue of Peace. Do not write anything during this time. Merely begin your time by praying, "You,

Lord, are a God of peace. The Presence of the Holy Spirit is marked by peace. Show me where I am not at peace within myself or with others. Show me others not at peace with each other. Guide me, Lord, into being a peacemaker in these situations. Make me always aware of peace and its lack in my life. Amen."

At the end of your meditation time, ask yourself:

Do I want to be at peace with myself and all others or only with some others? What is preventing me from seeking or accepting peace? How might my life be if I were at peace with all? How can I foster that peace?

Find another section in Scripture which illustrates the Virtue of Peace. Find a statement of Jesus or an incident in His life that deals with the Virtue of Peace. Write these into your journal.

If you are a member of a Religious Order, find one place in your Rule or Constitutions which calls for the Virtue of Peace. Explain why you chose this section.

Practice the Virtue of Peace this week. Record in your journal any memorable insights or happenings.

Each evening, examine your day for the times when you did or did not practice peace, or when you did or did not sense a lack of peace around you. Pray each night, "Lord, help me to be at peace with myself, with You, and with all others. Show me how to do this. Give me the courage to try. Amen."

At the end of the week, record in your journal what you have learned from this exercise.

CHAPTER 34

Perseverance

Scripture

"Do not fear what you are about to suffer. Behold, the devil is about to throw some of you into prison, that you may be tested, and for ten days you will have tribulation. Be faithful unto death, and I will give you the crown of life." (Revelation 2:10)

Writings of Saint Francis

I, little brother Francis, wish to follow the life and poverty of Jesus Christ our Most High Lord and of His Most Holy Mother and to persevere therein until the end. And I beseech you all, my ladies, and counsel you, to live always in this most holy life and poverty. And watch yourselves well that you in no wise depart from it through the teaching or advice of any one. (Last wish which Saint Francis wrote to Saint Clare)

Incident from the Life of Saint Francis

When they saw him, his former acquaintances upbraided him with contempt, crying out to him as a mad man and one beside himself, and flung the mud of the streets and stones at him. For, perceiving him thus changed from his former ways, and worn out by mortification of the flesh, they imputed everything he did to want of food and madness. Nevertheless, the soldier of Christ passed himself through it all even as one deaf, neither broken down nor changed by any injury done him, but giving God thanks.

And when such a report of him had arisen in the places and streets of the city, it at last reached his father. But he, when he heard that such things were being done unto his son by his fellow-citizens, rose up forthwith to seek him, not that he might set him free, but rather that he might destroy him. For, setting no measure on his wrath, he ran upon him, driven as a wolf toward a sheep, with cruel and crafty countenance, and so laid lands in unfatherly wise upon him, dragging him into the house, where for many days he shut him up in a dark prison, endeavouring with words and stripes to bend back his mind unto the vanities of this world.

Nonethelesss was Francis moved neither by words, nor wearied out by stripes, bearing all patiently, and only endured thereby yet more eager for his holy purpose, and stronger to pursue it. (The Legend of the Three Companions, Chapter VI)

HOW MANY PEOPLE have you known who sign up to volunteer with great enthusiasm only to disappear after a session or two, or when the going gets tough? Perhaps you are that person. Many of the greatest accomplishments of the past centuries have been due to the perseverance of people who were dedicated to their cause.

Thomas Edison said, "Genius is 1% inspiration and 99% perspiration." He also is quoted as saying, when a worker lamented on lack of results in developing a nickel-iron battery, "Results! Why, man, I have gotten a lot of results! I know several thousand things that won't work."

Perseverance is keeping on keeping on, aiming for the goal, and not petering out or giving up. Saint Francis persevered in rebuilding three churches, mostly on his own and totally by hand, before people started to help him. When his first formal Rule was presented to the Pope, he had to write another. After painstaking months, the rewrite was carelessly lost by the Minister General and Francis had to write the Rule for the third time. After that Rule was approved, Francis persevered in living it to the end despite discord in his Order and grumbling by many against him and the Rule.

Keep on keeping on. Francis understood that well.

Spend a minimum of five minutes meditating on the Virtue of Perseverance. Do not write anything during this time. Merely begin your time by praying, "Lord, help me to understand the Virtue of Perseverance and where I need it in my life."

At the end of your meditation time, ask yourself: What are some of my accomplishments in life--getting through school, winning a contest, finishing a marathon? During these prolonged events, was I ever discouraged? Did I want to quit? What kept me going? How did I feel when I finally reached my goal or accomplished my objectives? Can I persevere under persecution? How can I increase my "perseverance quotient"?

Find another section in Scripture which illustrates the Virtue of Perseverance. Find a statement of Jesus or an incident in His life that deals with the Virtue of Perseverance. Write these into your journal.

If you are a member of a Religious Order, find one place in your Rule or Constitutions which calls for the Virtue of Perseverance. Explain why you chose this section.

Practice the Virtue of Perseverance this week. A good way to practice is to make a list of some of your spiritual weaknesses and vices and their opposite virtues. Choose one of them and make a list of activities you can implement to live out the opposite virtue, then persevere daily in it. For example, if you chronically show up late for daily Mass, try coming half an hour early for a week.

Each evening, examine your day for the times when you did or did not practice perseverance. Pray each night, "Lord, give me the Virtue of Perseverance so that I may follow through with my promises and good intentions. Transform me into a person who sees a job through to the end, all for Your greater glory, my Lord. Amen."

At the end of the week, record in your journal what you have learned from this exercise.

CHAPTER 35

Poverty

Scripture
The wisdom of a humble man will lift up his head, and will seat him among the great. Do not praise a man for his good looks, nor loathe a man because of his appearance. The bee is small among flying creatures, but her product is the best of sweet things. Do not boast about wearing fine clothes, nor exalt yourself in the day that you are honored; for the works of the Lord are wonderful and his works are concealed from men. Many kings have had to sit on the ground, but one who was never thought of has worn a crown. (Sirach 11:1-5)

Writings of Saint Francis
"Blessed are the poor in spirit: for theirs is the kingdom of heaven." Many apply themselves to prayers and offices, and practise much abstinence and bodily mortification, but because of a single word which seems to be hurtful to their bodies or because of something being taken from them, they are forthwith scandalized and troubled. These are not poor in spirit: for he who is truly poor in spirit, hates himself and loves those who strike him on the cheek. (Admonitions 14)

"And those who came to receive life gave all that they had to the poor and were content with one tunic patched inside and out, with a cord and trousers. And we did not wish to have more." (Testament)

Incident from the Life of Saint Francis
The blessed Francis with the other brethren repaired to a place called Rivo Torto by the city of Assisi. Here there was a forsaken hovel beneath whose shelter those most strenuous despisers of large and beautiful houses abode, and protected themselves from storms

of rain. For, as saith the Saint, one ascends to Heaven quicker from a hovel than from a palace. In that same place there dwelt with the blessed father all his sons and brethren in much toil and in lack of all things; very often, wholly deprived of the solace of bread, they were content with turnips only, which in their distress they begged for here and there over the plain of Assisi. Their dwelling was so extremely cramped that they could scarce sit down or rest in it. There was not a sound of murmuring or complaining at these things, but their heart being at peace their mind was filled with joy and kept them patient. . . .

He wrote the names of the brethren on the beams of the dwelling so that each if he wished to rest or pray might recognize his own place, and so that the painful smallness of the space might not cause the silence of the mind to be troubled. Now one day while they were staying there a man leading an ass chanced to come to the shelter where the man of God was dwelling with his companions, and in order not to be driven away, he urged his ass to go in, saying these words, "Go in, for we shall do good to this place." When St. Francis heard these words and perceived what the man meant, he was moved in spirit, for the man thought that the brethren intended to stay there [as owners] in order to enlarge the place, and "add, house to house." And St. Francis went out forthwith, and forsook that hovel, because of what the countryman had said, and he removed to another place not far from it called Portiuncula, where, as was said above the Church of St. Mary was that he had repaired long before. He would have nothing in the way of property that he might the more fully possess all things in the Lord. (The Life of Saint Francis by Thomas of Celano, Chapter XVI)

ST. BASIL SAID: "When someone steals another's clothes, we call them a thief. Should we not give the same name to one who could clothe the naked and does not? The bread in your cupboard belongs to the hungry; the coat unused in your closet belongs to the one who needs it; the shoes rotting in your closet belong to the one who has no shoes; the money which you hoard up belongs to the poor."

Saint Francis embraced this idea. As a young man, he was interested in the finest foods prepared in the most succulent ways and in wearing rich, lavish fabrics which his father sold through the family's cloth business. Nevertheless, Francis was always generous with the poor. He gave them alms and treated them courteously, but he never really identified with them. Living as the poor lived was the farthest thing from his mind until his conversion. Then Francis realized that "more means less, and less means more." He realized that he had become the slave of his pride and his possessions, and that, if he wanted freedom, he had to dispossess himself of both.

The Franciscan Virtue of Poverty means doing with as little as you need and keeping things simple. It also means being able to relinquish with an open hand whatever anyone wants or takes away. Those who have a spirit of poverty deal more patiently with loss, because they know that what they owned wasn't really theirs in the first place -- everything is a gift of God.

Jesus said "Blessed are the poor in spirit". He is referring to this openhanded attitude regarding everything we have including our reputation, our job, our home, our loved ones, and our time. Jesus is asking us to be humble enough to accept God's active and permissive will in every aspect of our lives. He calls us to continue to be faithful and loving toward our Creator no matter what happens in our worldly life.

Some people believe that poverty is a relative term. For instance, people whose income is under the poverty line in the United States live in relative luxury, as far as material things are concerned, compared to people in Third World countries. Mother Teresa once commented that people in the West have a different kind of poverty -- not only a poverty of loneliness but also of spirituality. There's a hunger for love, as well as a hunger for God.

Spend a minimum of five minutes meditating on the Virtue of Poverty. Do not write anything during this time. Merely begin by praying, "Lord, help me to understand the Virtue of Poverty and where I need it in my life."

At the end of your meditation time, ask yourself: Does poverty attract or repel me? Would I say that I am poor? Why or why not? If I have too many possessions, should I give some away? We always talk about increasing our income level. How can I increase my poverty level? What about a person's life style or possessions would make me label him or her a "poor" person? Do I agree with Francis' idea that voluntary poverty of possessions leads to spiritual wealth? Do I know any poor people? Have I ever admired or been inspired by a particular poor person? Why was that person a model for me?

Find another section in Scripture which illustrates the Virtue of Poverty. Find a statement of Jesus or an incident in His life that deals with the Virtue of Poverty. Write these into your journal.

If you are a member of a Religious Order, find one place in your Rule or Constitutions which calls for the Virtue of Poverty. Explain why you chose this section.

Practice the Virtue of Poverty this week. Begin by making a list of all your blessings (be sure to have at least ten). Each day look at your possessions and find one or more that you can do without. Give these to a thrift shop. At the end of the week, you may not be much poorer over all, but you will have made an effort to dispossess yourself of some of your "stuff." Do you feel that any grace came to you through this? At the same time, make an effort to practice poverty of spirit by responding virtuously to the bumps on the road of your life. These bumps are places to apply the virtues in this book.

Each evening, examine your day for the times when you did or did not practice the Virtue of Poverty. Pray each night, "Lord, I am too attached to my things and to my own will and self. Grant me a spirit of poverty so that I may declutter my physical surroundings and my mental attitudes. Grant me the freedom of an open heart and an open hand, Lord. Amen."

At the end of the week, record in your journal what you have learned from this exercise.

Chapter 36

Praise

Scripture

O Lord, Thou wilt open my lips: and my mouth shall declare Thy praise. (Psalm 1:17)

I will bless the Lord at all times, His praise shall be always in my mouth. (Psalm 34 [33]:1)

Writings of Saint Francis

And since He has suffered so many things for us and has done and will do so much good to us, let every creature which is in heaven and on earth and in the sea and in the abysses render praise to God and glory and honor and benediction; for He is our strength and power who alone is good, alone most high, alone almighty and admirable, glorious and alone holy, praiseworthy and blessed without end forever and ever. Amen. (Second Version of the Letter to the Faithful)

Incident from the Life of Saint Francis

So after he had rested for a few days in the place he had so greatly longed for, and knew that the time of death was imminent, he called to him two brethren, and his specially loved sons and bade them in exultation of spirit sing, with a loud voice praises to the Lord concerning death which was near, rather life which was so close at hand; while himself, as he was able, broke into that Psalm of David, "I cried unto the Lord with my voice, with my voice unto the Lord I made supplication." [Ps. 142:1] (The Life of Saint Francis by Thomas of Celano, Second Book, Chapter VIII)

WE OWE GOD everything! Why? Because God, Himself gave us everything … including His only Son, who died on a cross because of our sins. How do we not remember this? When we look around us and see the beauty of nature, the homes we live in, the food we eat, our families, etc., we should raise our eyes to heaven and give thanks and praise to God. Psalm 119 (118):164 says "Seven times a day I have given praise to Thee." Praise of God should never be far from our minds and should always be in our hearts and on our lips.

No matter what we suffer or how much we are filled with joy, we owe almighty God praise, honor and glory! We should praise Him not only for all He gives us, but also for all we suffer. If we offer praise while suffering, we are showing God that we truly love Him and understand that He will bring good out of that suffering!

A good place to begin is with the Psalms … They are full of praise!

Spend a minimum of five minutes meditating on the Virtue of Praise. Do not write anything during this time. Merely begin your time by praying, "Lord, help me to understand the Virtue of Praise and where I need it in my life."

At the end of your meditation time ask yourself:

Do I remember to thank God for all He has given me? Do I praise God often? Do I give God praise even when He allows me to suffer? Do I understand why it is so important to praise God often? Do I take time during different periods of the day to stop and say, "I love You Lord, I am thankful for Your great mercy, and I praise You with all of my mind, heart, and soul?" What can I do to give praise to God more often?

Find another section of Scripture which illustrates the Virtue of Praise. Find a statement of Jesus or an incident in His life that deals with the Virtue of Praise. Write these into your journal.

If you are a member of a Religious Order, find one place in your Rule or Constitutions which calls for the Virtue of Praise. Explain why you chose this section.

Practice the Virtue of Praise this week. Find ten things every day to praise God for. Then offer Him praise for them! Record these ten things, and any other memorable insights or happenings, in your journal.

Each evening, examine the day for the opportunities you had to show praise the Lord. Pray: "Lord, I know that I ask a lot of You in times of need and sometimes that is the only time I think about You. Grant me the grace of open eyes, that I may see all of the gifts and mercy which You have bestowed upon me. Make my heart a loving heart, that I may love You above all things. Most of all, fill my mind with praise for You, that You may be adored all the day long, every day of my life. Amen."

At the end of the week, record in your journal what you have learned from this exercise.

CHAPTER 37

Prayer

Scripture

"And this is the confidence which we have towards Him: 'That whatsoever we shall ask according to His will, He heareth us'." (1 John 5:14)

Writings of Saint Francis

Clerics are to perform the divine office according to the rite of the Roman Church, except for the Psalter, and they can have breviaries for that purpose. Laymen are to say twenty-four "Our Fathers" at matins; five at lauds; seven each at prime, terce, sext and none; twelve at vespers; and seven at compline. They should also pray for the dead. They should fast from the feast of all saints until Christmas. Those who voluntarily fast at Quadragessima, those forty days after Epiphany which the Lord consecrated with his own holy fasting, will themselves be blessed by the Lord; yet they are not required to do so if they do not want to. They must fast during Lent, but they are not required to do so at other times except on Fridays. In case of obvious necessity, however, they are excused from bodily fasting. (Later Rule, Chapter III)

Incident from the Life of Saint Francis

Francis the man of God had been taught to seek not his own things but those which he might perceive to be specially expedient for the salvation of others; but yet above all things he longed to be dissolved and to be with Christ. Wherefore his chiefest study was to be free from all the things that are in the world, lest the serenity of his mind might even for a moment be troubled by the taint of any dust. He made himself insensible to the din of all outward things; and, gathering up with all his might from every side the outward senses, and keeping the natural impulses in check, occupied himself with

God alone. "In the clefts of the rock" he built his nest, and "in a hollow of the wall" was his habitation. [Canticles 2:14] Surely in fruitful devotion did he roam round lonely (caelibes) dwelling-places, and, wholly emptied [of himself], rested long in the Savior's wounds. Accordingly he often used to choose out solitary places in order that he might therein wholly direct his mind to God; but yet, when he was that the time was favorable, he was not slothful in attending to business and in applying himself gladly to the salvation of his neighbors. For his safest haven was prayer, not prayer for one moment, not vacant or presumptuous prayer, but long-continued, full of devotion, calm and humble; if he began late he scarce ended with morning. Walking, sitting, eating and drinking, he was intent on prayer. He would often go alone by night to pray in churches which were deserted, or in lonely places, wherein, under the protection of God's grace, he got the better of many fears and distresses of mind. (The First Life of Saint Francis by Thomas of Celano, Chapter XXVII).

PRAYER IS ABSOLUTELY necessary for eternal salvation; not only does God demand it of us, but we should also demand it of ourselves if we wish to have a rich spiritual life and a soul filled with a peace that can't be found in this world.

Prayer can be a request that we would like God to fulfill, a thanksgiving for gifts and graces received, a heartfelt conversation about what troubles us, or an expression of sorrow for our sins. It can be a request for intercession by one of our beloved Saints, a rosary, or prayers we find in prayer books. It doesn't matter what kind of prayer, where we are, what we are doing, if we are sitting, standing, kneeling, or laying down. What matters is that we pray and remain confident that God will answer us according to His will.

The content of our prayer also matters. God ALWAYS hears our prayers. Many times we think He ignores us or just doesn't care because our prayers have not been answered … or at least we think they haven't! The problem is that we tend to ask for things that aren't good for us or things that would damage our souls or cause us to sin. NO … God isn't going to answer the way you want Him to if it is not His Will for you. He will not grant anything that will cause harm to your soul.

Traditionally the Church recognizes four types of prayer: Petition, Adoration, Thanksgiving, and Praise. We should try to incorporate all of those types into our prayer life, every day if possible. A simple way to do that is to pray a prayer something like, "Lord, I give You my life and I ask for Your grace to live for You. [Petition] I adore Your marvelous might and wondrous beauty. [Adoration] Thank You for all You have given and all You have taken away. [Thanksgiving] I praise the magnificent wisdom in which Your Love rules the universe. [Praise] Amen."

We are told to "pray without ceasing" [1 Thessalonians: 17]. The Divine Office, or Liturgy of the Hours, is the prayer of the Church. It is very beautiful and is prayed 7 times a day. It can teach us to pray constantly. Also, the holy Rosary is a powerful weapon against evil and a wonderful prayer of intercession to our Blessed Mother.

No matter how we choose to pray, we can rest assured that our prayer will be heard. Additionally, if you combine fasting with prayer you will find strength and perseverance. You will find a peace of soul not of this world. You will be more aware of the fact that God has heard you, and He has indeed answered you. You will see miracles!

Spend a minimum of five minutes meditating on the Virtue of Prayer. Do not write anything during this time. Merely begin your time by praying, "Lord, help me to understand the Virtue of Prayer and where I need it in my life."

At the end of your meditation time, ask yourself:

How often do I pray? Do I ask for the right things, or do I ask for material things that I don't need or that would draw me away from God? Do I tend to rush through my prayer time so I can get back to the world, or do I focus on God and really have a conversation with Him? Do I listen to what God is saying to me, or do I get angry because I think He doesn't care? Am I ashamed to pray in open places, or do I love God enough to show Him that only He matters? Last of all, if I am in a crowd, do I excuse myself to take time out to pray, or do I just shrug it off so I don't miss anything?

Find another section in Scripture which illustrates the Virtue of Prayer. Find a statement of Jesus or an incident in His life that deals with the Virtue of Prayer. Write these into your journal.

If you are a member of a Religious Order, find one place in your Rule or Constitutions which calls for the Virtue of Prayer. Explain why you chose this section.

Practice the Virtue or Prayer this week by spending at least ten minutes a day in prayer. If you are already praying ten minutes or more per day, try to make your usual prayer time more meaningful by paying better attention to your prayers, by changing your normal prayer position, or by selecting some unfamiliar prayers. In your ten-minute prayer time, you may simply voice your prayers to God or use written prayers such as novenas or litanies. You may wish to intercede for someone, or you may wish to pray a Rosary or chaplet. Record in your journal any memorable insights or happenings.

Each evening, examine the day for the opportunities you had to enter into Prayer. Pray: "Lord, I ask that You teach me how to pray. Help me to overcome my worldly wants and to focus only on what will feed my soul. Teach me how to listen to Your answers and how to accept what is not pleasing to me, but is pleasing to You. Teach me to love You with all of my heart, mind, and soul, so that I will continually look to You during the day in prayer with all of my needs, my thanksgiving, and my praise. Teach me to pray … All for Thee, Lord, all for Thee! Amen."

At the end of the week, record in your journal what you have learned from this exercise.

CHAPTER 38

Presence

Scripture

As they led him away, they seized a man, Simon of Cyrene, who was coming from the country, and they laid the cross on him, and made him carry it behind Jesus. A great number of the people followed him, and among them were women who were beating their breasts and wailing for him." (Luke 23:26-27)

Writings of Saint Francis

Blessed is the person who supports his neighbor in his weakness as he would want to be supported were he in a similar situation. (Admonitions, XVIII)

Incident from the Life of Saint Francis

Blessed Francis went there to stay with his companion. But when he wanted to sleep there on the first night, demons came and beat him severely. He immediately called his companion who was staying some distance away. "Come to me." He got up at once and came to him. "Brother," blessed Francis told him, "the demons have beaten me severely so I want you to stay next to me because I am afraid to stay here alone. His companion stayed by him the whole night for blessed Francis trembled all over like a man suffering a fever. Both of them remained awake that whole night. (The Assisi Compilation, Section117)

WE DON'T OFTEN think of Presence as a Virtue, but certainly it is one. Consider Christ on the way to Calvary. Simon of Cyrene and the women of Jerusalem were present to Christ in His agony. At the foot of the cross stood the beloved disciple John, Mary Magdalen, and Jesus' mother. The presence of these faithful people, among the jeers and cruelty of the crowd and the soldiers, could not ease

Jesus's physical suffering, but their presence comforted Him and supported Him through His Passion.

Mother Teresa of Calcutta founded her Order on the Virtue of Presence. The Missionaries of Charity often can't heal the poor and dying, but they can always be present to them with love and compassion. The presence of love sweetens suffering.

Presence requires time which is why we often put off practicing this virtue unless it is thrust upon us. If we have a sick child, we need to care for that child, and the child, by crying and fretting, makes his or her needs known. We have to be present to bring the child food or medicine, to read a book or play a game. However, family and friends who are ill in a hospital or who reside in a long term care facility are not always "in our face." So we can easily over look them or make excuses for not being present to them.

The Virtue of Presence means more than just being with other people. You can be with many other people in a restaurant, movie theater, or mall and not be present to any of them. Presence means attention to the other person. Presence tells someone that you care about them, because you took time to be with them. Everyone deserves to benefit from the Virtue of Presence. Presence acknowledges the worth of the other person. Presence is a manifestation of love.

Spend a minimum of five minutes meditating on the Virtue of Presence. Do not write anything during this time. Merely begin your time by praying, "Lord, help me to understand the Virtue of Presence and where I need it in my life."

At the end of your meditation time, ask yourself:

Do I believe that God is always present to me? Do I want to be present to others? Am I comfortable being present to others? How do I feel if I can't "do" something to help someone else? Do I think presence with someone is enough?

Do I like people to be present to me? If so, when? If not, why not? How can I be more present to others?

Find another section in Scripture which illustrates the Virtue of Presence. Find a statement of Jesus or an incident in His life that deals with the Virtue of Presence. Write these into your journal.

If you are a member of a Religious Order, find one place in your Rule or Constitutions which calls for the Virtue of Presence. Explain why you chose this section.

Practice the Virtue of Presence this week. If you can't physically be with someone, how about a phone call where you can be audibly present? Record in your journal any memorable insights or happenings.

Each evening, examine your day for the times when you practiced being present to others. Was anyone present to you this week? Pray each night, "Lord, enhance my awareness of when I can and should be present to someone else. Give me courage to take time out of my busy day to be present to others. Amen."

At the end of the week, record in your journal what you have learned from this exercise.

CHAPTER 39

Purity

Scripture

Blessed are the pure in heart for they shall see God. (Matthew 5:8)

Writings of Saint Francis

"Blessed are the clean of heart: for they shall see God." They are clean of heart who despise earthly things and always seek those of heaven, and who never cease to adore and contemplate the Lord God Living and True, with a pure heart and mind. (Admonition 16)

Incident from the Life of Saint Francis

St. Francis most carefully examined himself and his companions daily, nay continually; he suffered not that any bit of wantonness should linger in them, and drove away all negligence from their hearts. Rigid in discipline he guarded himself watchfully at every hour, for if ever (as is usual) any fleshly temptation assailed him he would plunge in winter into a pit full of ice and remain there until all fleshly taint withdrew from him. And the others most eagerly followed the example of such mortification. (The Life of Saint Francis by Thomas of Celano, Chapter XVI)

PURITY MEANS FREEDOM from adulteration or contamination. The modern world is concerned about purity of water, air, and food but sometimes lax about purity of motive or behavior. Jesus, on the other hand, was concerned about purity of motive and behavior ("Blessed are the pure in heart," he said) and not so concerned about purity of physical substances. The Pharisees objected to His disciples eating with unwashed hands, thus ritually contaminating their food. Jesus noted that what goes into your mouth can't make you unclean. Instead, what contaminates a soul is what proceeds from the heart (meaning the free will) of a person and then comes out of the mouth. "For out of the heart come evil intentions, murder, adultery, fornication, theft, false witness, slander" (Matthew 15:19). We could add foul language, anger, sarcasm, hatred, and a host of other evil things to these.

How can we be pure? Keeping the Ten Commandments is a good way to begin. The Ten Commandments are:

I am the LORD your God. You shall worship the Lord your God and Him only shall you serve.
You shall not take the name of the Lord your God in vain.
Remember to keep holy the Sabbath day.
Honor your father and your mother.
You shall not kill.
You shall not commit adultery.
You shall not steal.
You shall not bear false witness against your neighbor.
You shall not covet your neighbor's wife.
You shall not covet your neighbor's goods.

The Catechism of the Catholic Church explains each commandment in depth and details what the commandment actually entails. For example, the Catechism has 72 brief sections on what falls under the fifth commandment. Actions discussed include homicide, suicide, war, abortion, scandal, drug abuse, health concerns, research involving human life at any stage, organ donation, kidnapping, hostage taking, care for the dead, hatred, anger, and legitimate defense.

Purity involves both motives and actions. It begins with keeping our thoughts on God and His moral laws. This is why purity is most commonly thought of in relationship to sexual thoughts and behavior. A pure person retains respect for the sexuality of themselves and others and relegates sexual activity to a sacramental marriage that is open to procreation. A pure person avoids pornography, suggestive language, and sexual self-stimulation as well as sexual activity outside of a sacramental marriage. Sexual purity was written into the Rule of Saint Francis and was required of all his followers. Purity of motive goes far beyond this, however. We are to seek out sincerity in all we think, say, and do. A reading of Saint Francis' Rule will reveal many instances where he enjoins purity of motive on his friars.

Spend a minimum of five minutes meditating on the Virtue of Purity. Do not write anything during this time. Merely begin your time by praying, "Lord, help me to understand the Virtue of Purity. Where do I have this virtue in my life? Where am I lacking it? Open my eyes to myself so that the Virtue of Purity may flourish in me."

At the end of your meditation time, ask yourself: Where does my life exhibit purity? Where does it exhibit impurity? Are my motives pure? Do I perform good actions for their own sake or because they will enhance my reputation? Do I believe purity is desirable? Why or why not? What can I do to strengthen the Virtue of Purity in my life or in society?

Find another section in Scripture which illustrates the Virtue of Purity. Find a statement of Jesus or an incident in His life that deals with the Virtue of Purity. Write these into your journal.

If you are a member of a Religious Order, find one place in your Rule or Constitutions which calls for the Virtue of Purity. Explain why you chose this section.

Practice the Virtue of Purity this week. Record in your journal any memorable insights or happenings.

Each evening, examine your day for the times when your purity of motive or deed was challenged. How did you meet this challenge? Could you have done better? How? Is there any way to rectify anything that lacked of purity today?

If so, make an effort to do this. Pray each night, "Lord, grant me the Virtue of Purity in my thoughts, motives, words and deeds. I know that this grace comes by Your help alone. Please grant this to me. Amen."

At the end of the week, record in your journal what you have learned from this exercise.

CHAPTER 40

Respect For Creation

Scripture

God saw all that he had made, and it was very good. And there was evening, and there was morning--the sixth day. (Genesis 1:31)

Writings of Saint Francis

Praised be You, my Lord, with all Your creatures,
especially Sir Brother Sun,
Who is the day and through whom You give us light.
And he is beautiful and radiant with great splendor;
and bears a likeness of You, Most High One.
Praised be You, my Lord, through Sister Moon and the stars,
in heaven You formed them clear and precious and beautiful.
Praised be You, my Lord, through Brother Wind,
and through the air, cloudy and serene, and every kind of weather,
through whom You give sustenance to Your creatures.
Praised be You, my Lord, through Sister Water,
who is very useful and humble and precious and chaste.
Praised be You, my Lord, through Brother Fire,
through whom You light the night,
and he is beautiful and playful and robust and strong.
Praised be You, my Lord, through our Sister Mother Earth,
who sustains and governs us,
and who produces various fruit with colored flowers and herbs. (Canticle of the Creatures)

Incident from the Life of Saint Francis

He spares lanterns, lamps, and candles, unwilling to use his hand to put out their brightness which is a sign of the eternal light.

He walked reverently over rocks, out of respect for Him who is called the Rock. When he came to the verse "You have set me high upon the rock," in order to express it more respectfully, he would say, "You have set me high under the feet of the Rock."

When the brothers are cutting wood, he forbids them to cut down the whole tree, so that it might have hope of sprouting again.

He commands the gardener to leave the edges of the garden undisturbed, so that in their season the green of herbs and the beauty of flowers may proclaim the beautiful Father of all. He even orders that within the garden a smaller garden should be set aside for aromatic and flowering herbs so that those who see them may recall the memory of the eternal savor.

He picks up little worms from the road so they will not be trampled underfoot.

That the bees not perish of hunger in the icy winter, he commands that honey and the finest wine should be set out for them.

He calls all animals by a fraternal name, although, among all kinds of beasts, he especially loves the meek. (The Remembrance of the Desire of a Soul by Thomas of Celano, Chapter CXXIV)

OF ALL THE virtues associated with Saint Francis, the one most commonly known is his respect for God's creation. How many of us have seen statues of Saint Francis holding a dove or sparrow, talking to a wolf, or surrounded by deer and rabbits? So prevalent are these representations that Saint Francis has jokingly been dubbed "the saint of the bird bath."

His actions and writings indicate Saint Francis's deep respect for every creature. He saw in each one the image of the Creator, and this image is what Francis reverenced in every created thing. How different would our lives be if each creature would recall to our minds the Creator?

The Virtue of Respect for Creation goes beyond recognizing God as Creator. The word "Respect" is operative. We respect—think highly of, are in awe of—creation because God created it. We are not careless with nor indifferent toward things that we think highly of; rather we care for them well. What possession do you regard highly? How do you treat it? We are to treat God's creation with the same concern.

Spend a minimum of five minutes meditating on the Virtue of Respect for Creation. Do not write anything during this time. Merely begin your time by praying, "Lord, help me to understand the Virtue of Respect for Creation. Show me how to do better, Lord."

At the end of your meditation time, ask yourself: Do I respect God's creation? If I were graded on my Respect for Creation, what would my grade be? How can I deepen my Respect for Creation? Would caring for a living thing, like a pet or a plant, help? Would taking a walk in a park or a garden help? Where can I find God in creation?

Find another section in Scripture which illustrates the Virtue of Respect for Creation. Find a statement of Jesus or an incident in His life that deals with the Virtue of Respect for Creation. Write these into your journal.

If you are a member of a Religious Order, find one place in your Rule or Constitutions which calls for the Virtue of Respect for Creation. Explain why you chose this section.

Practice the Virtue of Respect for Creation this week. At the very least, carry a small bag with you and begin by picking up trash that litters any area through which you walk. What other ways can you show Respect for Creation this week? Record in your journal any memorable insights or happenings.

Each evening, examine your day for times when you were aware of God through His creation. Did you praise God for His creative genius? Pray each night, "Lord, grant me the Virtue of Respect for Creation. Help me to see You through Your creation, to treat Your creation with dignity and awe, and to love You more because I see more clearly Your Divine Fingerprint. Amen."

At the end of the week, record in your journal what you have learned from this exercise.

CHAPTER 41

Sacrifice

Scripture

For I desire mercy, not sacrifice, and acknowledgment of God rather than burnt offerings. (Hosea 6:6)

Writings of Saint Francis

Consider, O man, how great the excellence in which the Lord has placed you because He has created and formed you to the image of His beloved Son according to the body and to His own likeness according to the spirit. And all the creatures that are under heaven serve and know and obey their Creator in their own way better than you. And even the demons did not crucify Him, but you together with them crucified Him and still crucify Him by taking delight in vices and sins. Wherefore then can you glory? For if you were so clever and wise that you possessed all science, and if you knew how to interpret every form of language and to investigate heavenly things minutely, you could not glory in all this, because one demon has known more of heavenly things and still knows more of earthly things than all men, although there may be some man who has received from the Lord a special knowledge of sovereign wisdom. In like manner, if you were handsomer and richer than all others, and even if you could work wonders and put the demons to flight, all these things are hurtful to you and in nowise belong to you, and in them you cannot glory; that, however, in which we may glory is in our infirmities, and in bearing daily the holy cross of our Lord Jesus Christ. (Admonition 5)

Incident from the Life of Saint Francis

But who now takes on himself Francis's concern for subjects? He always raised his hands to heaven for the true Israelites, attending first to his brothers' health and often

137

forgetting his own. Casting himself at the feet of Majesty he offered sacrifice of spirit for his sons, urging God to give generous gifts.

For the little flock which he drew behind him he felt compassion and love filled with fear, that after losing the world, they would also come to lose heaven. He thought he would be without future glory unless he could make those entrusted to him glorious along with him. His spirit had given birth to them with greater labor pains than a mother feels within herself. (The Remembrance of the Desire of a Soul by Thomas of Celano, Chapter CXXXII)

SACRIFICE, OR A variation of that word, is mentioned over three hundred times in Scripture. The Jewish temple was the scene of continuous sacrifices made to God. Bulls, sheep, doves, cereal, and the first fruits of the harvest were all sacrificed to God. What were the point of these?

The sacrifices were like the ancient Jewish collection envelope. People gave of their means and sustenance to God, and not just of their means but of the best they had. The Jewish laws forbid people to sacrifice blemished or imperfect animals because to do so was to give God the left overs, the stuff no one else wanted.

The word sacrifice is related to the Latin word *sacer* which means "holy." A sacrifice was something holy, something important or valued which one relinquishes for the sake of something more important or more valuable. The Jewish people sacrificed the first fruits of their fields and the first born of their livestock to God as a prayer asking the Lord to bless them with more than they gave to Him. Isn't this what we do today? We sacrifice something good for something better.

If we feel no pain in giving, have we made a sacrifice? A sacrifice involves the death of something, and death brings pain. We don't have to kill a sheep to make a sacrifice. If we give up time to help someone, or if we give to the soup kitchen what we could have had for supper, then we have died to our own wishes. That's a sacrifice, something at least a little bit painful.

Spend a minimum of five minutes meditating on the Virtue of Sacrifice. Do not write anything during this time. Merely begin your time by praying, "Lord, help me to understand the Virtue of Sacrifice and where I need it in my life."

At the end of your meditation time, ask yourself:

What sacrifices do I make daily, weekly, monthly, or yearly? Do I make these willingly or do I complain? Are there other sacrifices I should be making? What are they? How can I make them? What was the value of Jesus' sacrifice? What good comes from my sacrifices?

Find another section in Scripture which illustrates the Virtue of Sacrifice. Find a statement of Jesus or an incident in His life that deals with the Virtue of Sacrifice. Write these into your journal.

If you are a member of a Religious Order, find one place in your Rule or Constitutions which calls for the Virtue of Sacrifice. Explain why you chose this section.

Practice the Virtue of Sacrifice this week by purposely giving up something good to gain something greater. For example, you might sacrifice some time to offer a Rosary for someone who is ill or lonely or going through a difficult time. You might bake or purchase a lovely cake and then take it to a soup kitchen. Could you extra alms to your parish? Try to make at least one sacrifice each day. Record in your journal any memorable insights or happenings.

Each evening, examine your day for the times when you were able to make a sacrifice. Did you follow through? If not, why not? Pray, "Lord, give me the desire to sacrifice. Give me opportunities to sacrifice. Help me to understand the value of this marvelous virtue, not only for me but for others as well. Amen."

At the end of the week, record in your journal what you have learned from this exercise.

CHAPTER 42

Self- Knowledge

Scripture

I considered my ways and turned my feet to Your testimonies. (Psalm 119:59)

Writings of Saint Francis

Blessed is the servant who does not regard himself as better when he is esteemed and extolled by men than when he is reputed as mean, simple, and despicable: for what a man is in the sight of God, so much he is, and no more. (Admonitions 20)

Incident from the Life of Saint Francis

For oftentimes while all men were paying him honor he was wounded by exceeding grief, and, casting out the favor of men, he would, contrariwise, get someone to rebuke him. He would call one of the brethren to him and say, "On your obedience I bid you revile me harshly and tell me the truth in opposition to the lies of these men." And when that brother, though unwillingly, called him a boor, and a venal and unprofitable wretch, he would answer smiling and heartily applauding him, "The Lord bless you, because you are saying what is most true, for such things it is meet for the son of Peter di Bernardone to hear." Speaking thus he would recall his humble origin.[37]

54. And that he might perfectly show himself to be contemptible, and afford to the rest an example of true confession, he was not ashamed, when he had offended in anything, to confess it when he was preaching, before all the people. Nay more, if he chanced to have any evil thought about anyone, or happened to let fall an angry word, he would straightway confess the sin to him against whom he had thought or said anything evil, and beg his pardon. His conscience (witness of all innocence) guarded itself with all solicitude and did not let him rest until soothing words had healed the mental wound. Assuredly in his noteworthy deeds of every kind he craved not notoriety but profit, avoiding admiration by every means that he might never fall into vanity. (The Life of Saint Francis by Thomas of Celano, Chapter XIX)

HAS ANYONE EVER said to you, "Do you know what you are doing?" or "Don't you realize the impression you make on others?" Questions like this may indicate a lack of self-awareness (they may also indicate a lack of concern—I know what I'm doing and how I'm appearing to others, but I don't care.)

People can't advance in the spiritual life if they don't know themselves. We need to understand who we are, our good points and bad, our strengths and weaknesses, if we are serious about making spiritual progress. Saint Francis had a good barometer for self-knowledge: "for what a man is in the sight of God, so much he is, and no more." And, we might add, "so much is he and no less, too." We must always remember that we have great worth in the eyes of God Who loved us into being. We just might be diamonds in the rough or jewels covered with mud. We need some polishing and cleaning to bring out the beauty in our souls.

So how do you learn to know yourself? You can pray, think, discern, or read, but one of the easiest ways to know who you really are is to ask a person who will honestly tell you. Your children, spouse, parents, or trusted friend can give you tremendous, and sometimes painful, insights into yourself. How can you improve if you don't know where you need it?

Spend a minimum of five minutes meditating on the Virtue of Self-Knowledge. Do not write anything during this time. Merely begin your time by praying, "Lord, help me to understand myself, my motives, my sins, and my virtues. Let me be neither discouraged nor prideful. Amen."

At the end of your meditation time, ask yourself:

Who am I really? What do I find hardest to face about myself? Can I do anything about that? How? Who can help? What type of person do I wish I were? Is it possible to become like that? How?

Find another section in Scripture which illustrates the Virtue of Self-Knowledge. Find a statement of Jesus or an incident in His life that deals with the Virtue of Self-Knowledge. Write these into your journal.

If you are a member of a Religious Order, find one place in your Rule or Constitutions which calls for the Virtue of Self-Knowledge. Explain why you chose this section.

Practice the Virtue of Self-Knowledge this week by, each day, asking someone to tell you honestly what your strengths and weaknesses are. Ask them to suggest how you can improve. Instead of getting angry or embarrassed, simply thank your confidant and promise to think about what he or she told you.

Each day, write that day's insight and suggestions into your journal. Each evening, reread what the confidant told you that day. What insights do you get?

At the end of the week, compare what your confidants said. What common threads do you see? Are there any common suggestions? What might work for you? Make some changes in the direction of spiritual and moral improvement. Pray, "Lord, help me to know, accept, and love myself. Give me the courage to bolster my good qualities and eradicate my bad ones. Show me how, Lord, and grant me Your grace. Amen."

At the end of the week, record in your journal what you have learned from this exercise.

CHAPTER 43

Service

Scripture

"[W]hatever you did for one of the least of these brothers and sisters of mine, you did for me." (Matthew 25:40)

Writings of Saint Francis

To all Christians, religious, clerics, and laics, men and women, to all who dwell in the whole world, Brother Francis, their servant and subject, presents reverent homage, wishing true peace from heaven and sincere charity in the Lord.

Being the servant of all, I am bound to serve all and to administer the balm-bearing words of my Lord. . . . We should never desire to be above others, but ought rather to be servants and subject "to every human creature for God's sake." (Second Version of the Letter to the Faithful)

Incident from the Life of Saint Francis

Then the holy lover of profound humility moved to the lepers and stayed with them. For God's sake he served all of them with great love. He washed all the filth from them, and even cleaned out the pus of their sores, just says he said in his Testament: "When I was in sin, it seemed too bitter for me to see lepers, and the Lord led me among them and I showed mercy to them."(The Life of Saint Francis by Thomas of Celano, Chapter VII)

MOST PEOPLE DON'T have to look very far to find objects of service. The spiritual and corporal works of mercy are traditional ways to serve others.

The Spiritual Works of Mercy are:

Instruct the ignorant
Advise the doubtful
Correct sinners
Be patient with those in error or who do wrong
Forgive offenses
Comfort the afflicted
Pray for the living and the dead.

The Corporal Works of Mercy are:

Feed the hungry
Give drink to the thirsty
Clothe the naked
Shelter the homeless
Visit the sick and imprisoned
Ransom the captive
Bury the dead.

You can probably think of other ways to serve people. Service is best done with a joyful rather than a grumpy spirit, without expecting praise, and without necessarily even being asked. However, when you are in a situation where someone else is in authority, it is always wise to ask before performing a service. "Should I set the table?" "Would you like me to move that box for you?"

Jesus told us that He came to serve, not to be served. This should be the motto of anyone who is trying to develop the Franciscan virtues. Serving others is where the "rubber meets the road" in the spiritual life.

Spend a minimum of five minutes meditating on the Virtue of Service. Do not write anything during this time. Merely begin your time by praying, "Lord, help me to see how I can serve others. Give me the grace to serve graciously. Amen."

At the end of your meditation time, ask yourself:

Am I a server? Do I like to serve others or do I wait to be waited on? Do I see what needs to be done and pitch in, or do I wait to be asked? Do I look for ways to serve others? When I am asked to be of service, how do I respond? What is my response if I am asked to serve in a way that displeases me? How can I improve my "Service Rating"?

Find another section in Scripture which illustrates the Virtue of Service. Find a statement of Jesus or an incident in His life that deals with the Virtue of Service. Write these into your journal.

If you are a member of a Religious Order, find one place in your Rule or Constitutions which calls for the Virtue of Service. Explain why you chose this section.

Practice the Virtue of Service this week by, each day, looking for at least three ways to serve others and then performing the service without expecting acknowledgment.

Each evening, write in your journal the ways you served others that day. How do you feel about the times you served others? Pray, "Lord, You have given every good thing to me, so it is right that I give some of my time and resources and help to others. Show me ways to be of service to my brothers and sisters in this world. Develop in me a grateful attitude for being able to serve people in Your name. Amen.

At the end of the week, record in your journal what you have learned from this exercise.

CHAPTER 44

Silence

Scripture

But Jesus often withdrew to lonely places and prayed. (Luke 5:16)

Writings of Saint Francis

Those who want to remain in hermitages to lead a religious life should be three brothers, or four at most; of these, let two be "mothers" and have two "sons," or one at least.

The two that are "mothers" should maintain the life of Martha and the two "sons" the life of Mary, and have a single enclosure, in which each may have his cell to pray and sleep in.

And they are always to say Compline of the day immediately after sunset. And they should make sure to keep the silence. And they are to recite their Hours. And they are to get up for Matins. And let the first thing they seek be the kingdom of God and his justice.

. . . . And as to the enclosure where they stay, they may not allow any person either to enter or to eat there.

Those brothers who are the "mothers" are to make sure they keep their distance from people and, on account of the obedience due their minister, shield their "sons" from people, so that nobody can get to speak with them.

And those "sons" are not to speak with any person other than their "mothers" and their minister and custodian, when he wishes to visit them with the blessing of the Lord God. (Rule for Hermitages)

Incident from the Life of Saint Francis

I want to leave and bequeath to the brothers the place of Saint Mary of the Portiuncola as a testament, that it may always be held in the greatest reverence and devotion by the brothers. Our old brothers did this: for although the place itself is holy, they preserved its holiness with constant prayer day and night and by constant silence. And it, at times, they spoke after the time established for silence, they discussed with the greatest devotion and decorum matters pertaining to the praise of God and the salvation of souls. If it happened, and it rarely did, that someone began to utter useless or idle words, immediately he was corrected by another. (The Assisi Compilation, Chapter 56)

SILENCE IS A virtue in many ways. When we keep silent instead of saying something critical or hurtful that would've benefited no one, we have practiced the Virtue of Silence. When we let others speak and we listen without interrupting, we have practiced the Virtue of Silence. When we allow our minds to be alone with God, without interruption or distraction or noise, we have practiced the Virtue of Silence.

Do you like silence? Would you rather have noise and activity? Silence can be threatening because, in the silence, we have to confront our fears, our sins, and our needs without anything to distract us. This is why Jesus went to lonely places to pray. He had no distractions there to keep him from his focus on God.

Those who wish to follow Jesus need to have silence in their lives. They need to find a place where they can be alone with God and where He can speak to their heart without interruption from outside activity. Silence is a virtue, not in itself, but by what is accomplished when one is silent. One speaks to God. One allows others to speak. One refrains from speaking hurtful words. One lets God speak. Often, we have to work at maintaining silence or finding silence in our lives. How much silence does your life have?

Spend a minimum of five minutes meditating on the Virtue of Silence. Do not write anything during this time. Merely begin your time by praying, "Lord, help me to see the value of the Virtue of Silence. How can I find silence? How can I be silent? Enlarge my understanding, Lord. Amen."

At the end of your meditation time, ask yourself:

Do I see the value of silence? Am I naturally a quiet person? Do I know when to keep silence and when to speak? Do I ever pray before blurting out something? Do I like silence? Does silence make me uneasy? If so, what frightens me or unnerves me about silence? Have I ever sought silent time with God? Do I do all of the talking during my prayer time, or do I stop and listen to God? Do I have a place to go where I can be silent? Do I have a time of day when I can savor the silence? If not, where can I find these?

Find another section in Scripture which illustrates the Virtue of Silence. Find a statement of Jesus or an incident in His life that deals with the Virtue of Silence. Write these into your journal.

If you are a member of a Religious Order, find one place in your Rule or Constitutions which calls for the Virtue of Silence. Explain why you chose this section.

Practice the Virtue of Silence this week. Try to increase your awareness of when to speak and when to remain silent. Ask the Holy Spirit to help you with this discernment. Then carve out a time each day for 5 to 15 minutes of silence. Can you take this time early in the morning if you wake up 15 minutes earlier? Is there a quiet place—a church, a park, a parking lot—where you can go after work for this silent time (turn off your cell phone!)? Could you create a prayer closet in your home (it could be a cleared out closet) where you can close the door and have relative silence? Work at finding a place and making time. Then just be quiet with God. Don't worry about saying anything to God or fret if God says nothing to you. Every day, just savor the silence.

Each evening, write into your journal any insights you gained about the Virtue of Silence. Was it easy or difficult to keep silent? Are you becoming more comfortable with silence? What is silence teaching you? Pray, "Lord quiet my tongue and quiet my mind. Grant tranquility to my spirit. Let me feel Your Presence in the silence. Amen.".

At the end of the week, record in your journal what you have learned from this exercise.

CHAPTER 45

Simplicity

Scripture

At that time Jesus declared, "I thank You, Father, Lord of heaven and earth, that You have hidden these things from the wise and understanding and revealed them to little children." (Matthew 11:25)

Writings of Saint Francis

"Blessed are the poor in spirit: for theirs is the kingdom of heaven." Many apply themselves to prayers and offices, and practise much abstinence and bodily mortification, but because of a single word which seems to be hurtful to their bodies or because of something being taken from them, they are forthwith scandalized and troubled. These are not poor in spirit: for he who is truly poor in spirit, hates himself and loves those who strike him on the cheek. (Admonitions 14)

Incident from the Life of Saint Francis

This man not only hated pretense in houses; he also abhorred having many or fine furnishings in them. He disliked anything in tables or dishes, that recalled the ways of the world. He wanted everything to sing of exile and pilgrimage. (The Assisi Compilation, Section 24)

SIMPLICITY DOES NOT mean simple minded. Lacking mental acuteness or shrewdness is a quality of mind, not a virtue. The Virtue of Simplicity means the quality or condition of being easy to understand or do. Simplicity is freedom from complexity, intricacy, deceit, guile, or division. It is the absence of luxury, pretentiousness, and ornament. You might say that simplicity is getting down to the basics. What would those basics be in the spiritual life? They would be unfailing faith in God and surrender to him.

St. Francis is often known for his poverty, but simplicity would be the all-encompassing virtue of his life. Francis saw everything as following Christ. He reduced his entire Rule of Life to following the Gospel. The only book that matter to him was the Bible. He wanted his friars to have the least amount of possessions and clothing as necessary. Simplicity extended even to obeying the superior in all things that were not sinful and seeing that obedience as surrender to God.

And, indeed, simplicity fosters surrender to God. The more things we have, the more things we do, the more responsibilities we undertake, the more complex our life becomes, the less time we have for spending with God. The fewer things we have to worry about, the freer our life becomes. We are available to serve God moment by moment however life unfolds before us. This is living in simplicity.

Those who live in the world as lay men and women have responsibilities that those in religious life do not have. This means that laity have to struggle to maintain or establish simplicity in their lives. However, we can all cultivate greater simplicity. As we simplify, we will discover more peace because we will have fewer things, worries, and responsibilities cluttering our minds. We will find that we can hear God speak to us when our minds are less cluttered and what He says may be revealing! Simplicity is a virtue precisely because it opens us up to God.

Spend a minimum of five minutes meditating on the Virtue of Simplicity. Do not write anything during this time. Merely begin your time by praying, "Lord, show me the value of simplicity in my life. Show me how to simplify my life. Grant me the desire for this virtue. Amen."

At the end of your meditation time, ask yourself:

Would I call my life simple? What is the basis of my answer? How can I simplify my life in the following areas: clothing, possessions, activities, responsibilities, recreation, work, duty parenting? How can I improve my attitude and actions in the areas of my life that I simply cannot simplify?

Find another section in Scripture which illustrates the Virtue of Simplicity. Find a statement of Jesus or an incident in His life that deals with the Virtue of Simplicity. Write these into your journal.

If you are a member of a Religious Order, find one place in your Rule or Constitutions which calls for the Virtue of Simplicity. Explain why you chose this section.

Practice the Virtue of Simplicity this week by simplifying your life in one of the areas mentioned above. Let's suppose you chose the parenting category. How can you simplify your parenting? Can you teach your children to eat what you cook rather than trying to prepare several meals for several different tastes? Can you teach your children to dress themselves and to keep track of their chores (or begin doing chores)? Are there any children's activities that you can cut out of your schedule? Can you implement guidelines to make parenting run more smoothly in your family? Try some of these things and then keep on doing what works. Record in your journal any memorable insights or happenings.

Each evening, examine your day for the times when you were able to simplify your life in some way. Did you do it? If not, why not? Pray each night, "Lord, I know that my life needs to be simplified. If I had a simpler life, I would have more time for You. Show me how to simplify my life, Lord. Give me the courage to do what You show me. Amen."

At the end of the week, record in your journal what you have learned from this exercise.

Chapter 46

Surrender

Scripture
Submit yourselves therefore to God. Resist the devil, and he will flee from you. (James 4:7)

Writings of Saint Francis
The Lord says in the Gospel: he "that doth not renounce all that he possesseth cannot be" a "disciple " and "he that will save his life, shall lose it." That man leaves all he possesses and loses his body and his soul who abandons himself wholly to obedience in the hands of his superior, and whatever he does and says—provided he himself knows that what he does is good and not contrary to his [the superior's] will—is true obedience. And if at times a subject sees things which would be better or more useful to his soul than those which the superior commands him, let him sacrifice his will to God, let him strive to fulfil the work enjoined by the superior. This is true and charitable obedience which is pleasing to God and to one's neighbor.

If, however, a superior command anything to a subject that is against his soul it is permissible for him to disobey, but he must not leave him [the superior], and if in consequence he suffer persecution from some, he should love them the more for God's sake. For he who would rather suffer persecution than wish to be separated from his brethren, truly abides in perfect obedience because he lays down his life for his brothers. 1 For there are many religious who, under pretext of seeing better things than those which their superiors command, look back and return to the vomit of their own will. These are homicides and by their bad example cause the loss of many souls. (Admonitions 3)

Incident from the Life of Saint Francis

*Then he came before the bishop and was received by him with great joy. "Your father,"
the bishop said to him, "is infuriated and extremely scandalized. If you wish to serve
God, return to him the money you have, because God does not want you to spend
money unjustly acquired on the work of the church. [Your father's] anger will abate
when he gets the money back. My son, have confidence in the Lord and act coura-
geously. Do not be afraid, for He will be your help and will abundantly provide you
with whatever is necessary for the work of his church."*

*Then the man of God got up, joyful and comforted by the bishop's words, and, as
he had brought the money to him, he said: "My Lord, I will gladly give back not only
the money acquired from his things, but even all his clothes." And going into one of the
bishop's rooms, he took off all his clothes, and putting the money on top of them, came
out naked before the bishop, his father, and all the bystanders, and said: "Listen to me,
all of you, and understand. Until now I have called Pietro di Bernardone my father.
But, because I have proposed to serve God, I returned to him the money on account of
which he was so upset, and also all the clothing which is his, wanting to say from now on:
'Our Father who are in heaven,' and not 'My father, Pietro de Bernardone..'" At that
moment, the man of God was found to be wearing under his colored clothes a hairshirt
next to his skin. (The Legend of the Three Companions, Chapter VI)*

THE VERB SURRENDER has three meanings:

Give up or agree to forego to the power or possession of another
Relinquish possession or control over
Relinquish to the power of another; yield to the control of another

These are precisely the definitions which apply to the Virtue of Surrender.

We generally think of surrender in terms of war or power struggle. We imagine that surrender is a desperate attempt, made as a last resort, to save one's life
or the lives of others as in a war. Immediately following surrender, we imagine
torture and prison for the one surrendering. No wonder surrender has a bad image in the common view.

However, as St. Francis and all the saints learned, the secret of sanctity lies in surrender. We need to surrender our will, our way of doing things, our wants, and our possessions to God, and we need to let God take over our lives and give us what He wants. We need to do this if we wish to be holy because God, being infinitely powerful and all knowledgeable, knows precisely what will perfect us. We may totally disagree with His tactics, but then God knows us far better than we know ourselves. He knows what is best for us, what we need to become holy. So we have to stop fighting God and let Him work.

How holy do you want to become? Do you want to go straight to heaven when you die, or are you happy to be purified in Purgatory, where you will learn to surrender all? If you can achieve perfect surrender in this life, you will be perfectly ready for the next. However, we do not often recognize our attachments. Every attachment to person, place, thing, opinion, desire, or comfort has to be surrendered to God with an open hand, allowing Him to take away anything and everything if He deems it best for us. That is surrender.

Spend a minimum of five minutes meditating on the Virtue of Surrender. Do not write anything during this time. Merely begin your time by praying, "Lord, show me where I need to surrender to You. Give me the grace to do this. Amen."

At the end of your meditation time, ask yourself:

Did my meditation make me uncomfortable? What and who am I not willing to part with? Am I afraid of what God will do if I surrender to Him? If I am afraid of surrender to God, what does this reveal about my faith in Him? Do I believe that God will make all things work to my good? What good would that be? Am I courageous enough to ask God for the Virtue of Surrender?

Find another section in Scripture which illustrates the Virtue of Surrender. Find a statement of Jesus or an incident in His life that deals with the Virtue of Surrender. Write these into your journal.

If you are a member of a Religious Order, find one place in your Rule or Constitutions which calls for the Virtue of Surrender. Explain why you chose this section.

Practice the Virtue of Surrender this week. Every day, give up something you wanted as a practice. Perhaps refrain from a snack, turn on a television show five minutes late, or donate above what you normally would to the parish collection basket. Record these daily into your journal. Pray, "Lord, I want to surrender my life to You. Jesus, take over!" Record in your journal any memorable insights or happenings.

Each evening, examine your day for the times when you were able to surrender your will or possessions. Pray each night, "Lord, strengthen the Virtue of Surrender in me. Give me the courage to truly give You everything I am and have. Amen."

At the end of the week, record in your journal what you have learned from this exercise.

CHAPTER 47

Trust

Scripture

"BLESSED IS THE man who trusts in the Lord, whose trust is the Lord. He is like a tree planted by water, that sends out its roots by the stream, and does not fear when heat comes, for its leaves remain green, and it is not anxious in the year of drought, for it does not cease to bear fruit." (Jeremiah 17:7, 8)

Writings of Saint Francis

O OUR most holy FATHER,
Our Creator, Redeemer, Consoler, and Savior
WHO ARE IN HEAVEN:
In the angels and in the saints,
Enlightening them to love, because You, Lord, are light
Inflaming them to love, because You, Lord, are love
Dwelling in them and filling them with happiness,
*   because You, Lord, are the Supreme Good,*
*   the Eternal Good*
*   from Whom comes all good*
*   without Whom there is no good.*

HALLOWED BE YOUR NAME:
May our knowledge of You become ever clearer
That we may know the breadth of Your blessings

the length of Your promises
the height of Your majesty
the depths of Your judgments

YOUR KINGDOM COME:
So that You may rule in us through Your grace
and enable us to come to Your kingdom
where there is an unclouded vision of You
a perfect love of You
a blessed companionship with You
an eternal enjoyment of You. (Prayer Inspired by the Our Father)

Incident from the Life of Saint Francis

At the same time also the entrance of another good man into the Religion raised their number to eight. Then blessed Francis called them all together to him, and after saying many things to them concerning the Kingdom of God, the despising of the world, the renouncing their own will and the subjection of their own bodies, he divided, them by twos into four parts and said to them, "Go, dearest brethren, two and two through different parts of the world, announcing to men peace, and repentance for remission of sins; and be patient in tribulation, sure that the Lord will fulfill His purpose and promise. To those who question you answer humbly, bless them that persecute you, give thanks to them that revile and slander you, because for these things an eternal kingdom is preparing for us." And, they accepting the injunction of holy obedience with joy and great gladness, fell down humbly on the ground before St. Francis. But he embraced them affectionately and earnestly and said to each one, "Cast thy thought on the Lord and He will nourish thee." These words he used to say whenever he sent any brethren away on an "obedience." (The Life of Saint Francis by Thomas of Celano, Chapter 11)

TRUST IN GOD may just be the most difficult thing to do when it comes to faith! How is it possible to put trust in someone we can't see, have never met, and who seems silent most of the time? Yet, this is exactly what we are asked to do.

In order to trust fully in God, we must become as little children. "Amen, I say to you, whosoever shall not receive the kingdom of God as a little child shall not enter into it." (Mark 10:15) We must trust God as a child trusts his or her parents. Through prayer, fasting, and mortification of the senses, we can become like children and will begin to fully trust in God.

Jesus had total trust in God when He was in the garden and He prayed: "My Father, if it be possible, let this chalice pass from me. Nevertheless, not as I will, but as Thou wilt." (Matthew 26:39) Mary had total trust in God when she said "be it done to me according to thy word." (Luke 1:38). Joseph had total trust in God when he took Mary as his wife despite the fact they had never been intimate, yet Mary was with child. There are many examples of trust in Scripture.

Saint Francis instructed his followers to speak humbly when questioned, to bless their persecutors, to thank those who reviled and slandered them, and to trust that the Lord would nourish them. How is this possible, considering our human nature is to do the exact opposite? If we have total trust in God, we will not waver when faced with trials. Instead, we will accept those trials with patience and without fear. We will bear fruit because God will shine in us. Let us trust in God and bring Him souls!

Spend a minimum of five minutes of meditation on the Virtue of Trust. Do not write anything during this time. Merely begin by praying, "Lord help me to understand the Virtue of Trust and where I need it in my life."

At the end of your meditation ask yourself:

When I pray, do I pray with confidence and trust that God will answer my prayer? Do I trust that God will answer in a way that will best benefit my soul? Do I accept the trials God allows, trusting that He knows best and will bring good out of what seems harmful and painful? Do I pray, fast, and mortify my senses in order to build total trust in God? Do I strive to become childlike so that I can trust God as a child trusts his or her father?

Find another section in Scripture which illustrates the Virtue of Trust. Find a statement of Jesus or an incident in His life that deals with the Virtue of Trust. Write these into your journal.

If you are a member of a Religious Order, find a place in your Rule or Constitutions which calls for the Virtue of Trust. Explain why you chose this section.

Each evening, examine the day for the opportunities to show Trust. Did you have a time, or several times, during your day when you had to trust God, yourself, or others? Were you able to trust in these circumstances? Why or why not? Pray, "Lord, I tend to trust in myself and others, which brings nothing but turmoil into my life. Teach me how to become like a child and have total confidence in You alone. Grant me the grace needed to totally abandon myself to Your care, knowing that trust in You will bring me peace of soul, will allow me accept all trials without hesitation, and will help me to bring You souls. For Your greater honor and glory, Lord, teach me to trust in You. Amen."

At the end of the week, record in your journal what you have learned from this exercise.

CHAPTER 48

Vigilance

Scripture

Be sober and watch: because your adversary the devil, as a roaring lion, goes about seeking whom he may devour. (1 Peter 5:8)

Writings of Saint Francis

And let them remember what the Lord says: "and take heed to yourselves, lest perhaps your hearts be overcharged with surfeiting and drunkenness, and the cares of this life: and that they come upon you suddenly. For as a snare shall it come upon all that sit upon the face of the whole earth." (First Rule, Chapter IX)

Incident from the Life of Saint Francis

Another time, after his return from overseas, he went to Celano to preach; and a certain knight invited him very insistently, with humble devotion, to dine with him. So he came to the knight's home and the whole family delighted at the arrival of the poor guests. Before they took any food, the man offered prayers and praise to God as was his custom, standing with his eyes raised to heaven. When he had finished his prayer, he called his kind host aside and confidently told him: "Look, brother host, overcome by your prayers, I have entered your home to eat. Now heed my warnings quickly because you shall not eat here but elsewhere. Confess your sins right now, contrite with the sorrow of true repentance; and leave nothing in you unconfessed that you do not reveal in a true confession. The Lord will reward you today for receiving His poor with such devotion." The man agreed to the saint's words without delay; and telling all of his sins in confession to his companion, he put his house in order and did everything in his power to prepare for death. Then they went to the table; and while the others began to eat, suddenly their host breathed forth his spirit, carried away by sudden death according to the words of the man of God. (The Major Legend of Saint Francis by Saint Bonaventure, Chapter 11)

MOST OF US have forgotten why God made us. He made us to know, love, and serve Him in this world and to be happy with Him in the next. Many people think the only goal in this life is to please themselves. It doesn't matter to them if the pleasures they experience are offending God and even cutting them completely off from Him. Most think that they have all the time in the world to worry about death. Live now … pray and fast later. Confess next week, next month, or next year! Do not confess at all to a priest because "God knows my sins … I have confessed to God!"

How we need the example that Saint Francis has set for us! He has reminded us that we never know when we are going to leave this world. We need to live every day of our lives as though it was the last one. That means we should pray and fast and prepare ourselves for death. As the Scripture says "Be sober and watch: because your adversary the devil, as a roaring lion, goes about seeking whom he may devour." (1 Peter 5:8) If we are not vigilant, we will easily fall prey to the devil. Just one day with mortal sin on our soul can deprive us of that happiness with God that we so desire.

So be vigilant! Pray, fast, confess your sins and avoid the near occasions of sin so that you are never unprepared to go home to God! As Jesus said, "You know neither the day nor the hour." Be vigilant!

Spend a minimum of five minutes meditating on the Virtue of Vigilance. Do not write anything during this time. Merely begin your time by praying. "Lord, help me to understand the Virtue of Vigilance and where I need it in my life."

At the end of the meditation time, ask yourself:

Do I do sinful things without giving God a thought? Do I think I will have time later to confess and repent or do I understand that my life could end at any moment and I may not have time to prepare my soul? Do I pray continually and do penance for my sins, knowing that I may not have much time? More importantly, do I love God enough to keep watch on my soul so that I will never be without Him in this world or the next?

Find another section in Scripture which illustrates the Virtue of Vigilance. Find a statement of Jesus or an incident in His life that deals with the Virtue of Vigilance. Write these into your journal.

If you are a member of a Religious Order, find one place in your Rule or Constitutions which calls for the Virtue of Vigilance. Explain why you chose this section.

Practice the Virtue of Vigilance this week. Try to stay alert for temptations that can make you fall spiritually. Make an examination of conscience each day before bedtime. If you discover any sins committed during the day, make a point of going to confession as soon as possible. Record in your journal any memorable insights or happenings.

Each evening, examine your day for the times when you were vigilant and for the times you lacked vigilance. Pray each night: "Lord, it is so easy to become distracted with the things of this world and to forget to keep watch over my soul. Help me always to be on guard: to pray and fast and hold tight to the thought of my heavenly reward, so that I may not lose my soul and may be ready when You call on me. Amen."

At the end of the week, record in your journal what you have learned from this exercise.

CHAPTER 49

Vulnerability

Scripture

I gave My back to those who struck Me,
And My cheeks to those who plucked out the beard;
I did not hide My face from shame and spitting.

"For the Lord God will help Me;
Therefore I will not be disgraced;
Therefore I have set My face like a flint,
And I know that I will not be ashamed. (Isaiah 50:6-7)

Writings of Saint Francis

I SPEAK TO you, as best I can, about the state of your soul. You must consider as grace all that impedes you from loving the Lord God and whoever has become an impediment to you, whether brothers or others, even if they lay hands on you. And may you want it to be this way and not otherwise. And let this be for you the true obedience of the Lord God and my true obedience, for I know with certitude that it is true obedience. And love those who do those things to you and do not wish anything different from them, unless it is something the Lord God shall have given you. And love them in this and do not wish that they be better Christians. And let this be more than a hermitage for you.

And if you have done this, I wish to know in this way if you love the Lord and me, His servant and yours: that there is not any brother in the world who has sinned-- however much he could have sinned -- who, after he has looked into your eyes, whatever depart without your mercy, if he is looking for mercy. And if he were not looking for mercy, you would ask him if he wants mercy. And if he would sin a thousand times before your eyes, love him more than me so that you may draw him to the Lord; and always be merciful with brothers such as these. (A Letter to a Minister)

Incident from the Life of Saint Francis

In order to show himself contemptible and to give others an example of true confession, when he did something wrong he was not ashamed to confess it in his preaching before all the people. In fact, if he had perhaps thought ill of someone or for some reason let slip a harsh word, he would go with all humility to the person of whom he had said or thought something wrong and, confessing his sin, would ask forgiveness. His conscience, a witness of total innocence, guarding itself with all care, would not let him rest and diligently heal the wound of his heart. And every type of praiseworthy deed he wished to be outstanding, but to go unnoticed. In every way he fled praise to avoid all vanity. (The Life of Saint Francis by Thomas of Celano, Chapter XIX)

MOST OF US dislike being vulnerable. When we are vulnerable, we are open to attack and wounding, whether physical, emotional, moral, or spiritual. Vulnerability is no virtue when it means that we are so weak morally or spiritually that we can fall into sin, agnosticism, ridicule, or disbelief. In the case of spiritual vulnerability, we need to practice the virtue of faith by praying and by educating ourselves on the teachings of Christ and the Church. If we are vulnerable to moral failings, we need to cultivate the virtues of fortitude and perseverance. The virtue of fortitude helps us to stand for what is right, and the virtue of perseverance helps us to persist in doing what is right. Vulnerability is not a virtue if it makes us open to wrong actions or beliefs.

It is, however, a virtue when it keeps us open to the feelings of others, for all are our brothers and sisters in Christ. What a blessing when others understand us and we understand them! Understanding comes from being vulnerable to whatever the other person shares with us or does to us.

A once popular song was entitled, "You always hurt the one you love." That indicates vulnerability. We need to be willing to be hurt if we are going to love and to serve. Many people begin to serve others, but as soon as they are criticized, corrected, or directed, they grow angry and give up their work of mercy. Vulnerability means continuing despite the wounds. Why do we continue to minister? We minister because we love the other more than we love our own comfort and self-esteem. We love the other enough to allow ourselves to be wounded by them even as we serve them.

Jesus, the Son of God, was made vulnerable to human beings. Ultimately, this vulnerability led to His Passion and death. St. Francis, in his desire to be like Christ, often made himself vulnerable to criticism when he accused himself of faults that he could have kept hidden, and when he accepted into the Order men whom others would consider unsuitable.

It may feel more secure to erect a wall of defense around our emotions so that no one and nothing can make us feel bad or harm us. However, this is not what Jesus did. He remained vulnerable. Love is always vulnerable. If we are to serve others, then only vulnerable love keeps our motives pure.

Mother Teresa of Calcutta reportedly wrote, on the wall of her home for children in Calcutta, a series of thoughts on vulnerability. Few people have expressed it better:

People are often unreasonable, irrational, and self-centered. Forgive them anyway.
If you are kind, people may accuse you of selfish, ulterior motives. Be kind anyway.
If you are successful, you will win some unfaithful friends and some genuine enemies. Succeed anyway.
If you are honest and sincere, people may deceive you. Be honest and sincere anyway.
What you spend years creating, others could destroy overnight. Create anyway.
If you find serenity and happiness, some may be jealous. Be happy anyway.
The good you do today, will often be forgotten. Do good anyway.

Give the best you have, and it will never be enough. Give your best anyway.
In the final analysis, it is between you and God. It was never between you and them
anyway.

Spend a minimum of five minutes meditating on the Virtue of Vulnerability. Do
not write anything during this time. Merely begin your time by praying, "Lord,
help me to understand the Virtue of Vulnerability and where I need it in my life."

At the end of your meditation time, ask yourself:

Am I vulnerable? If so, what makes me recognize this virtue in myself? If I
am not vulnerable, why not? Am I afraid of being vulnerable? Suppose that I am
vulnerable. What is the worst that can happen? What is the best that can happen?
Why did Jesus, our model in the spiritual life, make Himself vulnerable to weak
human beings?

Find another section in Scripture which illustrates the Virtue of Vulnerability.
Find a statement of Jesus or an incident in His life that deals with the Virtue of
Vulnerability. Write these into your journal.

If you are a member of a Religious Order, find one place in your Rule or
Constitutions which calls for the Virtue of Vulnerability. Explain why you chose
this section.

Practice the Virtue of Vulnerability this week. For example, risk paying a
compliment to someone who seems to dislike you. Work one day at a local soup
kitchen or homeless shelter. If someone asks you for money on the street, give
it to him or her. Ask someone whose opinion you respect to give you feedback
on a project that you have completed or are working on. Write a letter to the
newspaper on a controversial topic and present the Church's teaching regarding
it. Each of these activities, and many others, can make you vulnerable to criticism, misunderstanding, or rejection for doing what is right. "Do good anyway."

Each evening, examine your day for the times when you were vulnerable and the times when you found yourself putting up walls to avoid being hurt. Pray each night, "My God, make my soul vulnerable in good ways so that I may be docile to Your inspirations and deal with others in love no matter what the outcome may be. Help me to realize that service is between me and You, and what others think or say is not part of the equation. Amen."

At the end of the week, record in your journal what you have learned from this exercise.

Chapter 50

Wisdom

Scripture

For the LORD gives wisdom; from his mouth come knowledge and understanding. (Proverbs 2:6)

Writings of Saint Francis

Hail, Queen Wisdom! May the Lord protect You, with Your Sister, holy pure Simplicity! . . . Holy Wisdom confounds Satan and all his cunning. Pure holy Simplicity confounds all the wisdom of this world and the wisdom of the body. (A Salutation of the Virtues)

Incident from the Life of Saint Francis

Asking carefully and in detail about all their doings, he was always moved by a wholesome curiosity about all those in his charge. If he found something inappropriate was done, he did not leave it unpunished. He first discerned any spiritual vices. Then he judged those of the body, and finally uprooted any occasions that might open the way to sin. (The Life of Saint Francis by Thomas of Celano, Chapter XIX)

ALBERT EINSTEIN WROTE, "Wisdom is not a product of schooling but of the life-long attempt to acquire it."

Lao Tzu wisely advised, "To attain knowledge, add things every day. To attain wisdom, remove things every day." Both of these quotes attempt to say that wisdom and knowledge are two different things. Knowledge deals with facts. Wisdom deals with the soul. People may gain all the knowledge in the world, Jesus said, and still lose their souls. People with very little knowledge may be wiser than those who teach in universities. Often possessions, activities, and concerns impede the reception of Wisdom. Wisdom comes most easily when distractions are absent.

Wisdom, according to a dictionary definition, is the quality of having experience, knowledge, and good judgment. This is why a young person can be very knowledgeable but often is lacking in wisdom. They have not had enough experience to fully develop this virtue.

Wisdom deals with the things of God and His workings in the world and in eternity. Scripture tells us that God's ways are not human ways. Human ways are based on knowledge and prudence. God's ways are based on eternal wisdom, which is far superior to human knowledge and prudence. What can be more prudent than to try to understand, follow, and love Wisdom?

Wisdom is from God, and what better place to hear God's voice than the Bible? An entire book of Scripture is called the Book of Wisdom. Some theologians have identified the personification of Wisdom in this book with the second person of the Blessed Trinity, our Lord Jesus Christ. If we really want to understand God's Wisdom, we can begin with no better place than the Gospels. The Gospels explained to us the life of Christ, and we can see God's Wisdom at work in and through Him.

Spend a minimum of five minutes meditating on the Virtue of Wisdom. Do not write anything during this time. Merely begin your time by praying, "Lord, help me to understand the Virtue of Wisdom and where I need it in my life."

At the end of your meditation time ask yourself:

Would I consider myself wise? On the scale of Wisdom, where 1 is foolish and 10 is very wise, where would I rank myself? How can I gain wisdom? Am I gaining wisdom now? Where have I gained it in the past? How did it come about in my life? Do I need more wisdom? How might I go about attaining it?

What possessions, activities, and concerns may be impeding me from gaining Wisdom? What can I do about this?

Find another section of Scripture which illustrates the Virtue of Wisdom. Find a statement of Jesus or an incident in His life that deals with the Virtue of Wisdom. Write these into your journal.

If you are a member of a Religious Order, find one place in your Rule or Constitutions which calls for the Virtue of Wisdom. Explain why you chose this section.

Practice the Virtue of Wisdom this week. Begin by refusing to act impulsively. When you must make a decision, write down the pros and cons of various courses of action. This will give you knowledge about what to do. Then pray over what you have written and ask the Holy Spirit to show you what to do. You may also consult a spiritually mature person about your decision. Does the course of action which the Holy Spirit is suggesting to you seem prudent or not? If you know that God wants something of you, it is wise to do it no matter how humanly prudent it does or does not seem. Record any memorable insights or happenings from this week in your journal.

Each evening, examine the day for the opportunities you had to practice the Virtue of Wisdom. Pray, "Lord, grant me the grace to think as You do when making decisions and deciding on actions. I need Wisdom for certain situations in my life. Lord, grant me faith, courage, and wisdom. Amen."

At the end of the week, record in your journal what you have learned from this exercise.

CHAPTER 51

Witness

Scripture

If you declare with your mouth, "Jesus is Lord," and believe in your heart that God raised him from the dead, you will be saved. (Romans 10:9)

Writings of Saint Francis

Whenever it pleases them, all my brothers can announce this or similar exhortation and praise among all peoples with the blessing of God: Fear and honor, praise and bless, give thanks and adore the Lord God Almighty in Trinity and in Unity, Father, Son, and Holy Spirit, the Creator of all. Do penance, performing worthy fruits of penance because we shall soon die." (The Earlier Rule, Chapter XXI)

Incident from the Life of Saint Francis

He then began to preach penance to all with a fervent spirit and joyful attitude. He inspired his listeners with words that were simple and a heart that was heroic. His word was like a blazing fire, reaching the deepest parts of the heart, and filling the souls of all with wonder. He seemed entirely different from what he had been, and looking up to heaven he refused to look down upon earth. (The Life of Saint Francis by Thomas of Celano, Chapter X)

WITNESS MEANS TO see something or experienced something and then to give evidence of it. If we see or experience something but never reveal it, we have not given witness. Scripture asks us to witness to our belief in Jesus. We read in Scripture and in the lives of the saints the witness of many holy people who were not ashamed and not afraid to proclaim Jesus in their words and actions.

In many parts of the world, it is difficult and sometimes dangerous to witness to others our faith in Jesus Christ. Does this mean that people in those areas have no obligation to witness? No! It means that those people, indeed, all of us, should witness to Christ by our lives and, when prudent, by our words. One does not have to live in an area of the world that is hostile to Christianity in order to be in situations where it is imprudent to witness to Jesus. Jesus told us, "Do not cast your pearls before swine." This means that we pray about where, when, and what to say about Jesus. Some people and some environments are not receptive, and can be openly hostile, to witness about Christ. Talking about Jesus in these environments is like taking something precious and throwing it in the mud where the swine will trample it.

The best way to witness in these situations is by living and acting in a Christian manner. If someone notices why we are behaving differently than everyone else, we can then prudently ask a few questions and determine if the person is open to hearing about Jesus. If not, we can merely say, "My faith tells me that you are my brother (sister)."

Many times, we are afraid to witness because of criticism or rejection. Being made fun of for our faith is no reason to not witness to it. St. Francis was made fun of when he began his conversion, and he returned the curses and stones thrown at him by offering a blessing to his abusers. It took two years for people to realize that Francis was genuine, but, when they did, great conversions began.

Spend a minimum of five minutes meditating on the Virtue of Witness. Do not write anything during this time. Merely begin your time by praying, "Lord, help me to understand the Virtue of Witness and where I need it in my life."

At the end of your meditation time ask yourself:

Why is witnessing to God's love and actions important? Do I ever witness about our Lord? If I don't witness, can I verbalize the reasons why? How can I overcome my hesitation? How can I be a better witness to my faith? To whom should I witness? Can I think of any unique or unusual ways to witness? Do I consult the Catechism of the Catholic Church to clarify theological questions that may arise when I witness?

Find another section of Scripture which illustrates the Virtue of Witness. Find a statement of Jesus or an incident in His life that deals with the Virtue of Witness. Write these into your journal.

If you are a member of a Religious Order, find one place in your Rule or Constitutions which calls for the Virtue of Witness. Explain why you chose this section.

Practice the Virtue of Witness this week. Every day, make at least one opportunity to witness to your faith in Jesus Christ. For example, you may quietly bow your head and pray before eating a meal in public. You may give a "God Loves You" card (available from the Confraternity of Penitents Holy Angels Gift Shop, cfpholyangels.com) to a cashier. Perhaps you can explain a bit about Jesus to a child. You might offer to pray for and with someone who is troubled. Record any memorable insights or happenings from this week in your journal.

Each evening, examine the day for the opportunities you had to practice the Virtue of Witness. Pray, "Lord, make me a kind but determined witness of Your love. Give me opportunities to tell others about the marvelous things that You have done in my life and in the lives of others. Increase my ability to witness. Let the honorable way that I live my life be a continual witness to the Gospel of Jesus Christ. Amen."

At the end of the week, record in your journal what you have learned from this exercise.

Chapter 52

Work

Scripture

For even when we were with you, we gave you this rule: "The one who is unwilling to work shall not eat." (2 Thessalonians 3:10)

Writings of Saint Francis

And I worked with my hands, and want to do so still. And I definitely want all the other brothers to work at some honest job. Those who don't know how should learn, not because they want to receive wages but as an example and to avoid idleness. (Testament)

Incident from the Life of Saint Francis

Meanwhile, the holy man of God, having changed his habit and rebuilt that church, moved to another place near the city of Assisi, where he began to rebuild a certain church that had fallen into ruin and was almost destroyed. After a good beginning he did not stop until he had brought all to completion.

From there he moved to another place, which is called the "Portiuncola," where there stood a church of the Blessed Virgin Mother of God built in ancient times. At that time, it was deserted and no one was taking care of it. When the holy man of God saw it so ruined, he was moved by piety because he had a warm devotion to the Mother of all good and he began to stay there continually. The restoration of that church took place in the third year of his conversion." (The Life of Saint Francis by Thomas of Celano, Chapter IX)

TOO OFTEN TODAY we see work as a drudgery, but St. Francis saw it as a virtue. Taking his lead from the second letter to the Thessalonians, Saint Francis wanted his friars to work. In fact, the early friars were to work voluntarily without receiving any payment other than food. If they were not offered food for their work, and they had nothing to eat, then they were to beg for their sustenance.

The first men who followed Francis were allowed to keep their tools so that they could practice their trades. This way, they could assist people and be paid with meals instead of with money. Francis saw work as a way to do service while preventing the idleness that can cause a person to fall into temptation to sin.

Francis took Jesus as his model in all things, and Jesus worked—He learned the carpenter trade from His foster father Joseph. All work was acceptable to Francis except work that would increase the prestige of the friar or that could possibly be an occasion of sin to him or to others. We can imagine the early friars working in the fields, picking olives, carrying wood, building homes, and repairing sandals during the day while they retired to their friaries to pray at night. All the time they were working, the men were able to evangelize and witness to the people with whom they worked. We can take these hard working men as an example for ourselves who can also witness in our workplace to the role that Jesus plays in our lives.

Spend a minimum of five minutes meditating on the Virtue of Work. Do not write anything during this time. Merely begin your time by praying, "Lord, help me to understand the Virtue of Work and where I need it in my life."

At the end of your meditation time ask yourself:

What is my attitude toward work? Do I see work as a gift or a burden? How can I sanctify my work? Do I have enough to do or too little? Do my coworkers know that I am a Christian? Do I offer my work to God as a way to glorify Him? If my attitude toward work is poor, how can I improve it?

Find another section of Scripture which illustrates the Virtue of Work. Find a statement of Jesus or an incident in His life that deals with the Virtue of Work. Write these into your journal.

If you are a member of a Religious Order, find one place in your Rule or Constitutions which calls for the Virtue of Work. Explain why you chose this section.

Practice the Virtue of Work this week by sanctifying your work by offering it to God for His glory. Everyone has some work to do even those who are bedridden who may only be able to pray and to offer their sufferings to God. That kind of work is of the highest order. Whatever work do you do, whether paid or unpaid work, this week work patiently, diligently, and attentively. Look for the evidence of God in the work that you do. In that way, you will sanctify your work.

Each evening, examine the day for the times when you are able to make your work into a virtuous occupation. Pray, "Lord, I want to sanctify my work by doing it well for You. Help me to see the value of my work and to be grateful for being able to do it. Amen."

At the end of the week, record in your journal what you have learned from this exercise.

Conclusion

YOU HAVE FINISHED 52 weeks of study and practice on the virtues of Saint Francis.

Have they made a change in your life?

Are there any you need to re-practice?

Should you go through this book again and see how you have improved?

May Saint Francis intercede for you as you seek to become more closely united to Christ through the practice of the virtues in this book!

Made in the USA
San Bernardino, CA
23 October 2016